Kaplan Publishing are constantly finding new ways to make a difference to your studies and our exciting ~~~~~~~~ do offer something different to students looking ~~~~

D1103287

This book comes with free MyKaplan onlir ~~~~~~~ an study anytime, anywhere. **This free online resource is not sold separately and is included in the price of the book.**

Having purchased this book, y~~~~~~~~~~~~~~~~~~~~~~~~~~~~~~~.

CONTENT	AAT	
	Text	Kit
Electronic version of the book	✓	✓
Progress tests with instant answers	✓	
Mock assessments online	✓	✓
Material updates	✓	✓

How to access your online resources

Kaplan Financial students will already have a MyKaplan account and these extra resources will be available to you online. You do not need to register again, as this process was completed when you enrolled. If you are having problems accessing online materials, please ask your course administrator.

If you are not studying with Kaplan and did not purchase your book via a Kaplan website, to unlock your extra online resources please go to www.mykaplan.co.uk/addabook (even if you have set up an account and registered books previously). You will then need to enter the ISBN number (on the title page and back cover) and the unique pass key number contained in the scratch panel below to gain access. You will also be required to enter additional information during this process to set up or confirm your account details.

If you purchased through the Kaplan Publishing website you will automatically receive an e-mail invitation to MyKaplan. Please register your details using this email to gain access to your content. If you do not receive the e-mail or book content, please contact Kaplan Publishing.

Your Code and Information

This code can only be used once for the registration of one book online. This registration and your online content will expire when the final sittings for the examinations covered by this book have taken place. Please allow one hour from the time you submit your book details for us to process your request.

Please scratch the film to access your unique code.

Please be aware that this code is case-sensitive and you will need to include the dashes within the passcode, ~~~~~~ when entering the ISBN.

6585201

KAPLAN
PUBLISHING

AAT

AQ2016

ADVANCED DIPLOMA IN ACCOUNTING

Synoptic Assessment

EXAM KIT

This Exam Kit supports study for the following AAT qualifications:
AAT Advanced Diploma in Accounting – Level 3
AAT Advanced Certificate in Bookkeeping – Level 3
AAT Advanced Diploma in Accounting at SCQF – Level 6

KAPLAN PUBLISHING

British Library Cataloguing-in-Publication Data

A catalogue record for this book is available from the British Library.

Published by:

Kaplan Publishing UK

Unit 2 The Business Centre

Molly Millar's Lane

Wokingham

Berkshire

RG41 2QZ

ISBN: 978-1-78740-803-6

This Product includes content from the International Ethics Standards Board for Accountants (IESBA), published by the International Federation of Accountants (IFAC) in 2015 and is used with permission of IFAC.

CONTENTS

Features in this exam kit

In addition to providing a wide ranging bank of real exam style questions, we have also included in this kit:

- unit-specific information and advice on exam technique

- our recommended approach to make your revision for this particular unit as effective as possible.

You will find a wealth of other resources to help you with your studies on the AAT website:

www.aat.org.uk/

Quality and accuracy are of the utmost importance to us so if you spot an error in any of our products, please send an email to mykaplanreporting@kaplan.com with full details, or follow the link to the feedback form in MyKaplan.

Our Quality Co-ordinator will work with our technical team to verify the error and take action to ensure it is corrected in future editions.

SYNOPTIC ASSESSMENT

AAT AQ16 introduces a Synoptic Assessment, which students must complete if they are to achieve the appropriate qualification upon completion of a qualification. In the case of the Advanced Diploma in Accounting, students must pass all of the mandatory assessments and the Synoptic Assessment to achieve the qualification.

As a Synoptic Assessment is attempted following completion of individual units, it draws upon knowledge and understanding from those units. It may be appropriate for students to retain their study materials for individual units until they have successfully completed the Synoptic Assessment for that qualification.

All units within the Advanced Diploma in Accounting are mandatory. Four units are assessed individually in end of unit assessments, but this qualification also includes a synoptic assessment, sat towards the end of the qualification, which draws on and assesses knowledge and understanding from across the qualification:

- Advanced Bookkeeping – end of unit assessment

- Final Accounts Preparation – end of unit assessment

- Management Accounting: Costing – end of unit assessment

- Ethics for accountants – assessed within the synoptic assessment only

- Spreadsheets for Accounting – assessed within the synoptic assessment only

Summary of learning outcomes from underlying units which are assessed in the synoptic assessment

Underlying unit	Learning outcomes required
Advanced Bookkeeping	LO1, LO2, LO3, LO4, LO5
Final Accounts Preparation	LO1, LO2, LO3, LO4, LO5, LO6
Management Accounting: Costing	LO1, LO2, LO3, LO4, LO5
Ethics for Accountants	LO1, LO2, LO3, LO4, LO5
Spreadsheets for Accounting	LO1, LO2, LO3, LO4, LO5

FORMAT OF THE ASSESSMENT

The specimen synoptic assessment comprises five tasks and covers all five assessment objectives. Students will be assessed by computer-based assessment. Marking of the assessment is partially by computer and partially human marked.

In any one assessment, students may not be assessed on all content, or on the full depth or breadth of a piece of content. The content assessed may change over time to ensure validity of assessment, but all assessment criteria will be tested over time.

The following weighting is based upon the AAT Qualification Specification documentation which may be subject to variation.

	Assessment objective	Weighting
AO1	Demonstrate an understanding of the relevance of the ethical code for accountants, the need to act ethically in a given situation, and the appropriate action to take in reporting questionable behaviour	15%
AO2	Prepare accounting and VAT records and respond to errors, omissions and other concerns, in accordance with accounting and ethical principles and relevant regulations	15%
AO3	Apply ethical and accounting principles when preparing final accounts for different types of organisation, develop ethical courses of action and communicate relevant information effectively	15%
AO4	Use relevant spreadsheet skills to analyse, interpret and report management accounting data	25%
AO5	Prepare financial accounting information, comprising extended trial balances and final accounts for sole traders and partnerships, using spreadsheets	30%
	Total	100%

Time allowed: 2 hours and 45 minutes

PASS MARK: The pass mark for all AAT assessments is 70%.

 Always keep your eye on the clock and make sure you attempt all questions!

The detailed syllabus and study guide written by the AAT can be found at:

www.aat.org.uk/

ASSESSMENT OBJECTIVES

Assessment objective 1	Demonstrate an understanding of the relevance of the ethical code for accountants, the need to act ethically in a given situation, and the appropriate action to take in reporting questionable behaviour
Related learning objectives	**Ethics for Accountants** LO1 Understand the need to act ethically LO2 Understand the relevance to the accountant's work of the ethical code for professional accountants LO4 Identify action to take in relation to unethical behaviour or illegal acts
Assessment objective 2	Prepare accounting records and respond to errors, omissions and other concerns, in accordance with accounting and ethical principles and relevant regulations
Related learning objectives	**Ethics for Accountants** LO3 Recognise how to act ethically in an accounting role LO4 Identify action to take in relation to unethical behaviour or illegal acts **Advanced Bookkeeping** LO1 Apply the principles of advanced double-entry bookkeeping LO2 Implement procedures for the acquisition and disposal of non-current assets LO3 Prepare and record depreciation calculations LO4 Record period end adjustments **Final Accounts Preparation** LO2 Explain the need for final accounts and the accounting and ethical principles underlying their preparation LO3 Prepare accounting records from incomplete information
Assessment objective 3	Apply ethical and accounting principles when preparing final accounts for different types of organisation, develop ethical courses of action and communicate relevant information effectively
Related learning objectives	**Ethics for Accountants** LO3 Recognise how to act ethically in an accounting role **Final Accounts Preparation** LO1 Distinguish between the financial recording and reporting requirements of different types of organisation LO2 Explain the need for final accounts and the accounting and ethical principles underlying their preparation LO3 Prepare accounting records from incomplete information LO4 Produce accounts for sole traders LO5 Produce accounts for partnerships LO6 Recognise the key differences between preparing accounts for a limited company and a sole trader

Assessment objective 4	Use relevant spreadsheet skills to analyse, interpret and report management accounting data
Related learning objectives	**Management Accounting: Costing** LO1 Understand the purpose and use of management accounting within an organisation LO3 Apportion costs according to organisational requirements LO4 Analyse and review deviations from budget and report these to management LO5 Apply management accounting techniques to support decision making **Spreadsheets for Accounting** LO1 Design and structure appropriate spreadsheets to meet customer needs LO2 Use spreadsheet software to record, format and organise data
Assessment objective 5	Prepare financial accounting information, comprising extended trial balances and final accounts for sole traders and partnerships, using spreadsheets
Related learning objectives	**Final Accounts Preparation** LO4 Produce accounts for sole traders LO5 Produce accounts for partnerships **Advanced Bookkeeping** LO5 Produce and extend the trial balance **Spreadsheets for Accounting** LO1 Design and structure appropriate spreadsheets to meet customer needs LO2 Use spreadsheet software to record, format and organise data LO3 Use relevant tools to manipulate and analyse data LO4 Use software tools to verify accuracy and protect data LO5 Use tools and techniques to prepare and report accounting information

INDEX TO QUESTIONS AND ANSWERS

KAPLAN PUBLISHING

NOTE: The answers to the tasks in these scenarios can be found as spreadsheet files on your MyKaplan account (together with the text and word files required).

EXAM TECHNIQUE

- **Do not skip any of the material** in the syllabus.

- **Read each question** *very* carefully.

- **Double-check your answer** before committing yourself to it.

- Answer **every** question – if you do not know an answer to a multiple choice question or true/false question, you don't lose anything by guessing. Think carefully before you **guess**.

- If you are answering a multiple-choice question, **eliminate first those answers that you know are wrong.** Then choose the most appropriate answer from those that are left.

- **Don't panic** if you realise you've answered a question incorrectly. Getting one question wrong will not mean the difference between passing and failing.

Computer-based exams – tips

- Do not attempt a CBA until you have **completed all study material** relating to it.

- On the AAT website there is a CBA demonstration. It is **ESSENTIAL** that you attempt this before your real CBA. You will become familiar with how to move around the CBA screens and the way that questions are formatted, increasing your confidence and speed in the actual exam.

- Be sure you understand how to use the **software** before you start the exam. If in doubt, ask the assessment centre staff to explain it to you.

- Questions are **displayed on the screen** and answers are entered using keyboard and mouse. At the end of the exam, in the case of those units not subject to human marking, you are given a certificate showing the result you have achieved.

- In addition to the traditional multiple-choice question type, CBAs will also contain **other types of questions**, such as number entry questions, drag and drop, true/false, pick lists or drop down menus or hybrids of these.

- In some CBAs you will have to type in complete computations or written answers.

- You need to be sure you **know how to answer questions** of this type before you sit the exam, through practice.

KAPLAN'S RECOMMENDED REVISION APPROACH

QUESTION PRACTICE IS THE KEY TO SUCCESS

Success in professional examinations relies upon you acquiring a firm grasp of the required knowledge at the tuition phase. In order to be able to do the questions, knowledge is essential.

However, the difference between success and failure often hinges on your exam technique on the day and making the most of the revision phase of your studies.

The **Kaplan Study Text** is the starting point, designed to provide the underpinning knowledge to tackle all questions. However, in the revision phase, poring over text books is not the answer.

Kaplan Pocket Notes are designed to help you quickly revise a topic area; however you then need to practise questions. There is a need to progress to exam style questions as soon as possible, and to tie your exam technique and technical knowledge together.

The importance of question practice cannot be over-emphasised.

The recommended approach below is designed by expert tutors in the field, in conjunction with their knowledge of the examiner and the specimen assessment.

You need to practise as many questions as possible in the time you have left.

OUR AIM

Our aim is to get you to the stage where you can attempt exam questions confidently, to time, in a closed book environment, with no supplementary help (i.e. to simulate the real examination experience).

Practising your exam technique is also vitally important for you to assess your progress and identify areas of weakness that may need more attention in the final run up to the examination.

In order to achieve this we recognise that initially you may feel the need to practice some questions with open book help.

Good exam technique is vital.

THE KAPLAN REVISION PLAN

Stage 1: Assess areas of strengths and weaknesses

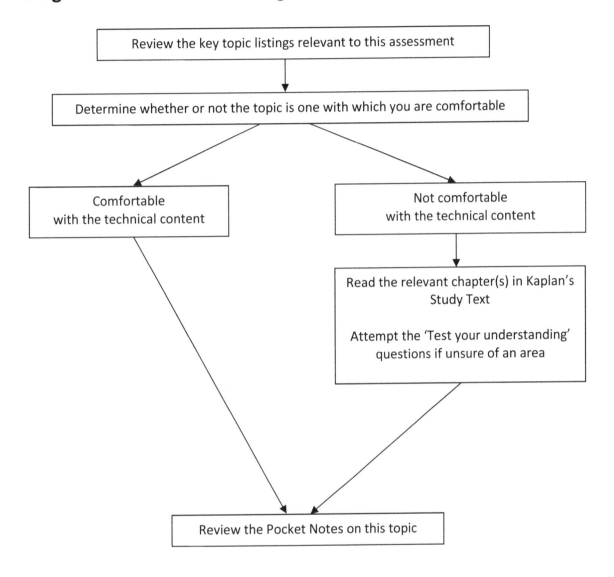

Stage 2: Practice questions

Follow the order of revision of topics as presented in this Kit and attempt the questions in the order suggested.

Try to avoid referring to Study Texts and your notes and the model answer until you have completed your attempt.

Review your attempt with the model answer and assess how much of the answer you achieved.

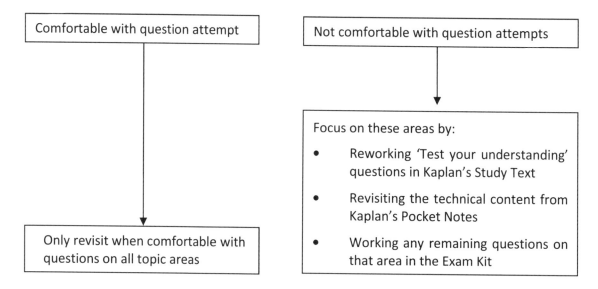

Stage 3: Final pre-exam revision

We recommend that you **attempt at least one mock examination** containing a set of previously unseen exam-standard questions.

Attempt the mock CBA online in timed, closed book conditions to simulate the real exam experience.

Section 1

EXAM – PART I – PRACTICE TASKS

ETHICS

TASK 1.1

Assessment objective 1	Demonstrate an understanding of the relevance of the ethical code for accountants, the need to act ethically in a given situation, and the appropriate action to take in reporting questionable behaviour

TASK 1.2

Assessment objective 2	Prepare accounting records and respond to errors, omissions and other concerns, in accordance with accounting and ethical principles and relevant regulations

TASK 1.3

Assessment objective 4	Apply ethical and accounting principles when preparing final accounts for different types of organisation, develop ethical courses of action and communicate relevant information effectively

1 FIVE SCENARIOS

Consider the following scenarios.

Scenario 1

Alessandro is an AAT member in practice employed by Sueka LLP. He has acquired some information about Polina Ltd in the course of acting for the company on an assurance engagement.

Complete the following sentence by selecting the appropriate option from the three options given below.

'The principle of confidentiality imposes an obligation on Alessandro to refrain from

using the information to the advantage of Sueka LLP'	
disclosing the information within Sueka LLP'	
disclosing the information to anyone at Polina Ltd'	

Scenario 2

Jacob, an AAT member in practice, is conducting a second interview of an excellent candidate (also an AAT member) for a senior post in Jacob's firm. When discussing remuneration the potential employee states she will bring a copy of the database of clients from her old firm to introduce new clients to Jacob's firm. She also says she knows a lot of negative information about her old firm which Jacob could use to gain clients from them.

Identify which of the following are the most appropriate actions for Jacob to take following the interview.

Because she shows business acumen, offer her the job	
Because she has breached the fundamental principles of integrity and confidentiality, report her to the AAT	✓
Because she lacks integrity, inform her that she will not be offered the job	✓

Scenario 3

Vernon, a member in practice, performs book-keeping services for both Yen Ltd and Piston Ltd. The two companies are in dispute about a series of purchases that Yen Ltd made from Piston Ltd.

Identify which fundamental ethical principles are threatened here from the options below.

Objectivity and confidentiality	
Integrity and professional behaviour	
Confidentiality and professional competence	

Scenario 4

Nick is a member in business. His cousin Sam has recently been employed by an organisation with which Nick has regular business dealings. Sam's position means that she would be able to offer Nick preferential treatment in the awarding of major contracts.

What should Nick do?

Nothing	
Seek legal advice	
Advise Sam of relevant threats and safeguards that will protect Nick should he receive such an offer from Sam's organisation	
Immediately inform higher levels of management	

Scenario 5

Conner, a member in practice, has just received a call from a potential new client asking him to help in a business transaction. However when asked for her address, the client said she would rather not say.

Advise Conner on how to respond to the client.

	Yes	No
Continue with forging a relationship with the client in the usual manner		✓
Inform the client that without knowing the correct address the client/ accountant relationship cannot be forged	✓	
Consider reporting the conversation to NCA	✓	

2   JESS

Jessica, a member in practice, has been tasked to complete an important assignment. However, she knows that she will not have enough time complete the work properly.

Indicate which fundamental ethical principle is under threat. Select ONE answer only.

Integrity	
Confidentiality	
Professional competence and due care	
Professional behaviour	
Objectivity	

3   NIGHT OUT

Bella, a professional accountant, was invited on a 'night out' with others from the accounts department. This became quite a boisterous evening and it ended with the Finance Director removing a sign from the front of a shop which he brought into the office the next day as a reminder of the good evening.

Required:

(a)   **Indicate which fundamental ethical principle is under threat. Select ONE answer only.**

Integrity	
Confidentiality	
Professional competence and due care	
Professional behaviour	
Objectivity	.

(b)   **Indicate what course of action Bella should take.**

Do nothing – a sign is not worth losing your job over	
Suggest to the FD that he should replace the sign	

4   DILEMMA

Your boss has told you that there are going to be some redundancies in the company. You will not be affected, but he has named a number of people who will be, including a good friend of yours who is in the process of buying a holiday home in Cornwall. You know that your friend would not be able to afford the property if she were to lose her job and that she would pull out of the purchase if she knew about the redundancy plans.

The news of the redundancies will not be made public for several weeks.

Required:

(a)   **Indicate which fundamental ethical principle is under threat. Select ONE answer only.**

Integrity	
Confidentiality	
Professional competence and due care	
Professional behaviour	
Objectivity	

(b)   **Indicate your best course of action**

From an ethical point of view you should tell your friend about the redundancies on the grounds it could save her unnecessary financial problems and distress.	
You should not tell your friend about the redundancies.	

5   JUSTIN

Justin is an AAT member in practice at Tipling LLP. He is a senior on an assurance assignment for Brittle plc. He inherits a 10% shareholding in this client.

Required:

(a)   **Which type of threat does this situation represent?**

Self-interest threat	
Self-review threat	
Intimidation threat	
Advocacy threat	
Familiarity threat	

(b)   **What would Justin's best course of action be?**

Continue as senior but make the partners aware of the inheritance	
Ask to be removed from the assignment	
Resign from Tipling LLP	
Report the matter to the National Crime Agency (NCA)	

6   PROCEDURE

Ye Lin, an AAT member, works for a C plc, a company that is now under investigation for corruption. The Finance Director has told Ye Lin not to cooperate with the investigation team.

Required:

(a)   **State whether Ye Lin should cooperate with the investigation or obey the FD.**

She should cooperate with the investigation	
She should refuse to cooperate as it would breach confidentiality	

(b)   **State what Ye Lin could be found guilty of if she fails to cooperate with the investigation.**

Misconduct	
Money laundering	
Whistleblowing	

(c)   **Indicate which of the following disciplinary actions the AAT could apply if Ye Lin is found guilty of damaging the reputation of the association. (Select all that apply)**

Lose her job with C plc	
Be expelled from the Association	
Have her membership of the Association suspended	
Have her practicing licence withdrawn.	
Receive a prison sentence	
Have to re-sit all her professional exams	

7   MLRO

Jeff, a member in practice has recently come across what he believes is an investigation by the regulatory authorities into allegations of money laundering at a large client.

Required:

(a)   **Jeff decides to communicate this to the Finance Director of the client. What offence Jeff will commit if he does this?**

Breach of confidentiality	
Tipping off	
Money laundering	

(b)   **What is the maximum sentence that Jeff can receive if found guilty of the offence.**

	Years

(c)   Jeff's defence includes the claim that his organisation does not have a MLRO (Money Laundering Reporting Officer). In the absence of an MLRO, who should Jeff have approached with his concerns?

HMRC	
The National Crime Agency (NCA)	
The national press	

(d)   A second part of Jeff's defence is that the amount in question was only £3,000 and that this is below the *de minimis* limit. What is the *de minimis* limit?

£	

8   DONNA

Donna, an accountant in practice, has recently been working on the tax computations for a client, Stoppard plc.

In preparing this year's tax returns Donna realised that she made an error preparing the last tax returns which resulted in an underpayment. She told the Finance Director of Stoppard plc about the error but he is refusing to tell the HMRC, claiming 'she made the mistake, not him'.

Indicate whether the following statements are true or false.

	True	False
Funds retained after discovery of a tax error amount to money laundering by Stoppard plc		
Donna should report the matter to the National Crime Agency (NCA)		
Donna needs to make an authorised disclosure to the National Crime Agency NCA		

9   CODE OF ETHICS

Indicate whether the following statements are true or false.

	True	False
An accountant is under no duty to disclose the limitations of their expertise to the client		✓
An accountant is only responsible for his or her own professional qualifications and training		✓
An accountant may need to compromise the most precise attention to detail in preparing work in order to meet a reasonable deadline		

10 INTEGRITY

Does an accountant breach his duty of integrity if the accountant: (tick all that apply)

Leaves a client to discover important information that is freely available?	✓
Only tells the client the information they have specifically asked for or that is habitually provided?	
Forgets to mention something important?	
Withholds information that may be compromising for the employer?	

11 CONFIDENTIAL

When might it be appropriate for an accountant to disclose information, provided in confidence?

A   At the request of the client

B   At the request of the regulator

C   At the request of a solicitor

D   At the request of the employer

12 THREATS

Classify the following threats according to the situations:

Self-interest threats	
Self-review threats	
Advocacy threats	
Familiarity threats	
Intimidation threats	

Preparing accounts for a campaign group of which the accountant is a leading member	
Preparing accounts under an unrealistically imposed deadline by a major client	
Preparing accounts for your close relative's business	
Preparing accounts for your spouse's business	F
Preparing accounts and providing a basic audit function on those accounts	ad.

13   E

E, a trainee management accountant, prepares an annual analysis of the performance of all staff, including her own. The analysis is used by the financial director to calculate staff bonuses each year.

According to the Code of Professional Ethics which of the threats listed below would apply to E?

A   Advocacy threat

B   Intimidation threat

C   Familiarity threat

D   Self-interest threat

14   R

R, a trainee management accountant is employed by JH. R has prepared the draft annual financial statements for JH and presented them to JH's Chief Executive prior to the executive board meeting. The Chief Executive has told R that the profit reported in the financial statements is too low and must be increased by £500,000 before the financial statements can be approved by the executive board.

Which of the threats listed below would apply to R in this situation, according to the Code of Professional Ethics?

A   Advocacy threat

B   Self-review threat

C   Intimidation threat

D   Self-interest threat

15   CX

CX, a professional accountant is facing a dilemma. She is working on the preparation of a long term profit forecast required by the local stock market listing regulations.

At a previous management board meeting, her projections had been criticised by board members as being too pessimistic. She was asked to review her assumptions and increase the profit projections.

She revised her assumptions, but this had only marginally increased the forecast profits.

At yesterday's board meeting the board members had discussed her assumptions and specified new values to be used to prepare a revised forecast. In her view the new values grossly overestimate the forecast profits.

The management board intends to publish the revised forecasts.

(a) **Which TWO of following ethical principles does CX face?**

A   Integrity

B   Confidentiality

C   Professional care and due competence

D   Objectivity

E   Professional behaviour

(b) **Place the following options into the highlighted boxes in the table below to correctly show the order CX should deal with an ethical dilemma.**

| Report internally to immediate management |
| Report externally |
| Remove herself from the situation |
| Gather evidence and document the problem |
| Report internally to higher management |

	Dealing with an ethical dilemma
1	
2	
3	
4	
5	

16   RS

RS, an employee, prepares monthly management accounting information for XYZ which includes detailed performance data that is used to calculate staff bonuses. Based on information prepared by RS this year's bonuses will be lower than expected.

RS has had approaches from other staff offering various incentives to make accruals for additional revenue and other reversible adjustments, to enable all staff (including RS) to receive increased or higher bonuses.

(a) **Which TWO of following ethical principles does RS face?**

A   Integrity

B   Confidentiality

C   Professional care and due competence

D   Objectivity

E   Professional behaviour

(b) **Which of following ethical threats does RS face?**

A   Advocacy threat

B   Self-review threat

C   Intimidation threat

D   Self-interest threat

17 PRINCIPLES

Match the principles from the Code of Professional Ethics in the list below to the relevant interpretation:

- Confidentiality
- Integrity
- Professional behaviour
- Professional competence and due care
- Objectivity

Principle	*Interpretation*
	Maintaining a relevant level of professional knowledge and skills so that a competent service can be provided.
	Complying with relevant laws and regulations.
	Being straightforward, honest and truthful in all professional and business relationships.
	Not disclosing information unless there is specific permission or a legal or professional duty to do so.
	Not allowing bias, conflict of interest or the influence of other people to override professional judgement.

18 ACTION

You are a management accountant working a UK listed chemical company. During the course of your duties, you become aware that the company is dumping waste illegally. You have raised this with your manager who has told you to ignore the issue.

Which of the following is NOT an appropriate course of action to take next?

A   Contacting AAT's ethical helpline for advice

B   Reporting the company to the environment agency

C   Contacting a journalist at a national newspaper

D   Taking the matter to the Audit committee

19 FUNDAMENTAL PRINCIPLES

The AAT Code of Ethics contains five fundamental principles of professional ethics for management accountants. Which of the following are fundamental principles, according to the Code? (Select ALL correct answers)

Confidentiality	✓
Honesty	✓
Objectivity	✓
Respect	
Integrity	✓

20 ETHICS AND LAW

Which of the following statement/s is/are correct?

If a person complies with the letter of the law she will always be acting ethically.	
Ethics in business is the application of ethical values to business.	
If a company has a code of ethics this will eliminate the need for legislation.	

21 ISSUES

Which of the following relates to an ethical issue?

A   The introduction of new IT systems to ensure the confidentiality of customers.

B   The recruitment of a new, highly qualified, finance director.

C   The purchase of larger more centrally located business premises to facilitate the expansion of the business.

D   The introduction of monthly reporting systems to maximise efficiency.

22 BREACHES

Which of the following statements are true?

You have been told that one of your colleagues in the accounts department has regularly submitted inflated expenses claims. This is a breach of the fundamental principle of integrity.	✓
You are aware that a colleague in the accounts department regularly takes home reports to check and does so after a few cocktails. This is a breach of the fundamental principle of professional behaviour.	
You are employed as Management Accountant and have been asked to dismiss one of your colleagues for misconduct. You are aware that this is untrue and that the Company is trying to reduce the workforce without making the due redundancy payments. This is a breach of the fundamental principle of integrity.	

23 AVOIDANCE

As part of the year end accounting procedures the Finance Director of Void Ltd is estimating the likely tax liability. As well as incorporating the finalised profit figure, the team involved are also looking at different ways of reducing the tax bill.

You are concerned that some of these methods may constitute tax evasion rather than tax avoidance.

Required:

Which of the following statements correctly explains the difference between tax evasion and tax avoidance?

Both tax evasion and tax avoidance are illegal, but tax evasion involves providing HM Revenue and Customs with deliberately false information.	
Tax evasion is illegal, whereas tax avoidance involves the minimisation of tax liabilities by the use of any lawful means.	✓
Both tax evasion and tax avoidance are illegal, but tax avoidance involves providing HM Revenue and Customs with deliberately false information.	
Tax avoidance is illegal, whereas tax evasion involves the minimisation of tax liabilities by the use of any lawful means.	

24 DUMPING

During your lunch you read an article in the FT about a case where a company was prosecuted through the courts for a breach of environmental laws regarding the dumping of toxic waste into drains, which subsequently lead to the open ocean. The case included testimony from the company's auditors which secured the prosecution.

You discussed this with one of the juniors who said that she thought that this would constitute a breach of confidentiality on behalf of the auditor.

Required:

Explain why this is not the case.

25 BENEFITS

Jacqui has recently been appointed as the chief accountant for a small public sector organisation. The other members of the senior management team (SMT) are very pleased with her appointment as they have really struggled to attract, recruit and retain good staff.

At the last meeting of the SMT it was decided that the benefits package for senior staff (including the SMT) was inadequate and that it needed revising.

Jacqui was asked to draw up the new package and, after considerable research and benchmarking, has decided that a significant increase is needed in the benefits package.

Required:

(a) Discuss which ethical principles are potentially compromised here.

(b) Identify which factors Jacqui should consider before making a decision what to do.

(c) Explain what the best course of action would be.

26   SUSHIL

Sushil is a member in business. His manager has asked him to falsify the accounts and has made it clear that if he refuses then he will lose his job.

Required:

(a) State which type of threat this situation represents.

(b)   Explain what the best course of action would be.

```
┌─────────────────────────────────────────────────────────┐
│                                                           │
│                                                           │
│                                                           │
│                                                           │
│                                                           │
│                                                           │
│                                                           │
│                                                           │
└─────────────────────────────────────────────────────────┘
```

27   TRUE

Naill is an AAT member working for a large building company. The finance director has asked him to adjust some of the sales figures, so that the year-end final numbers look better than they actually are.

Required:

(a)   Discuss whether Naill should do as the Finance Director instructs?

```
┌─────────────────────────────────────────────────────────┐
│                                                           │
│                                                           │
│                                                           │
│                                                           │
│                                                           │
│                                                           │
│                                                           │
│                                                           │
└─────────────────────────────────────────────────────────┘
```

(b)   Explain what is mean by 'false accounting'.

```
┌─────────────────────────────────────────────────────────┐
│                                                           │
│                                                           │
│                                                           │
│                                                           │
│                                                           │
│                                                           │
│                                                           │
│                                                           │
└─────────────────────────────────────────────────────────┘
```

28   MEERA

Meera works for a large accountancy firm as a tax specialist. Recently two matters have arisen:

Matter 1

On Monday Meera was in a meeting with a potential new client.

The potential client started by stating that he felt Meera's fees proposal was far too high and she needed to reduce them substantially.

He then said that he believed his tax bill for the previous year was also too high but if Meera guaranteed to reduce his tax bill, then he would come to her firm.

Meera had a quick look at the figures and she believed the sum looked reasonable.

(a)   **Explain what Meera should do in response to the client's requests.**

```



```

Matter 2

On Tuesday Meera had a dispute with Greg, a new client. After analysing Greg's tax affairs Meera had found a material error in the previous year's tax return that resulted in an underpayment of tax. The previous tax computations were prepared by Greg's previous accountant.

Meera advised Greg to tell HMRC about the error but so far he has refused to do so, claiming it is 'their problem, not his'.

(b)   **Should Meera tell HRMC about the error?**

```



```

(c)   **What should Meera do if Greg continues to refuse to inform the HMRC?**

```



```

29   RS

RS, an employee, prepares monthly management accounting information for XYZ which includes detailed performance data that is used to calculate staff bonuses. Based on information prepared by RS this year's bonuses will be lower than expected.

RS has had approaches from other staff offering various incentives to make accruals for additional revenue and other reversible adjustments, to enable all staff (including RS) to receive increased or higher bonuses.

(a)   **Which two ethical principles are threatened here?**

```



```

(b)   **What type of ethical threat does RS face?**

30   DISMISS

Sarah, a member employed in a division of a large building company, believes that one of the contract managers is attempting to short-cut building regulations by using substandard building materials in a new school.

Sarah has spoken to an internal whistle-blowing helpline about the situation and now the divisional manager is threatening to have her dismissed 'for not being a team player'.

Explain whether or not Sarah is protected by the PIDA (1998)?

31   MLC

MLC is a clothing retailer who imports clothes from diverse suppliers worldwide. MLC has a very strong, well-publicised corporate ethical code. The company accountant has just found out that one of MLC suppliers use child labour in the manufacture of their clothes and pay very low wages with cramped, dangerous conditions. This is in breach of contract conditions with that supplier.

This was raised at the last Board meeting and a wide range of opinions were discussed, including the following:

*   "Place more orders with the supplier – it's cheap labour so the margins are good, which should keep the shareholders happy."

*   "Leave things as they are and hope the information doesn't get out."

*   "Continue trading with the supplier but investigate the claims quietly."

*   "Cancel all contracts with the supplier and release a press statement stating how the company will always act quickly and decisively if unethical practices are suspected."

Advise the board.

```



```

32 STEPHANIE

Stephanie has worked in the finance department of Alpha for 5 years and has been promoted to work alongside the management accountant. Stephanie is currently working towards an AAT qualification.

The AAT-qualified management accountant of Alpha has told Stephanie that he works closely with department heads to produce their annual budgets. He is happy to allow significant 'slack' to be built in to these budgets to make them easier to achieve since, in his view, this makes Alpha a much more relaxed place to work.

Following this conversation, Stephanie overheard the management accountant agreeing to alter budgeted production figures to make them easier to achieve in return for tickets to a major football game. When she questioned her boss, he told her no harm was done since the budgeted figures are subjective anyway.

Discuss which ethical principles the management accountant is in breach of?

```



```

33 REFERENCE

Steve is a professional accountant working in practice.

Kept Ltd is Steve's oldest client and as well as the usual accountancy and tax services, Steve has recently been asked to write a reference to a new landlord confirming that Kept Ltd is likely to be able to pay its rent for the next 3 years.

While this would normally not be a problem, Steve is aware that Kept Ltd has been experiencing financial difficulties over the last 6 months, so he is wary of writing such a reference. To reassure him, the Chief accountant has offered to pay Steve a large fee for supplying the reference and suggested Steve should include a disclaimer of liability.

Required:

(a) **Analyse Steve's dilemma from an ethical point of view.**

(b) **If Steve writes the reference, knowing Kept Ltd may not be able to pay, what crime is he potentially committing?**

(c) **What difference would it make if Steve included a disclaimer of liability in the written reference?**

34 KUTCHINS

Gemma is an AAT member working for Kutchins Ltd, an engineering consultancy. She has recently started this job, having previously worked for an accountancy firm where she was the audit senior for Kirk Ltd, a competitor of Kutchins Ltd.

Required:

Explain whether Gemma is allowed to use knowledge, information and experience gained from her previous employer in her new job.

35 BEVIS

Bevis, an AAT member, has just joined a building company as a management accountant, after working for some years in a local accountancy practice.

The following situations have arisen in Bevis' first week at work.

Matter 1

When he first joined the company the Managing Director invited him out to lunch so that they could get to know each other. The Managing Director spent most of the time questioning Bevis about competitors who were clients of the firm Bevis used to work for.

Matter 2

As part of Bevis' work he needed to find out some information on behalf of the customer. When Bevis made the necessary phone call Bevis was told that the organisation did not have authority from the customer to disclose the information. When Bevis told his boss he told Bevis to ring back and pretend to be the customer.

Required:

Explain what Bevis should do in respect of the two matters above.

Matter 1

Matter 2

36 JULIE

Julie has audited the accounts of Believe It plc as part of the assurance team for the past five years. She has been approached by Believe It plc with an offer of the Senior Accountant role.

Required:

(a) State which type of threat this situation represent.

(b) Suggest TWO safeguards the assurance firm should have in place concerning such a threat.

Safeguard 1
Safeguard 2

37 NO DEFENCE

M plc is a large UK-based building firm that specialises in public sector contracts such as schools, hospitals and sports facilities.

Having a strong green and ethical reputation is vital to M plc's chances of winning government contracts. To protect its reputation, M has an internal ethics hotline for employees to raise any concerns they might have or evidence of wrongdoing.

Ever since the economic downturn in 2008, M plc has seen a major decline in its European business so the Board are keen to expand in other parts of the world.

Matter

In 2013 M plc was successful in winning a major contract to build new hospitals in Country H in Africa. However, a month later, the ethics hotline received a call concerning Mr Igbinadola, the agent who represented M plc in the negotiations with the government. The call claimed that Mr Igbinadola is well known for his excessive gifts and hospitality and paid for the MP involved in the negotiations to go on a lavish holiday just weeks before the contract was awarded. The Board of M plc claims no knowledge of such gifts and is adamant it didn't authorise this.

Required:

(a) Outline the four offences described by the UK Bribery Act 2010.

(b) Explain the defences a commercial organisation could offer to a charge of bribery.

(c) Discuss whether M plc could be guilty of an offence under the UK Bribery Act 2010.

38 L PLC

Andre, an AAT member, works for L plc, a UK company that exports a range of seed and other agricultural products to growers around the globe.

Recently Andre accompanied other representatives from L to go to a foreign country ('M') to discuss with a local farming cooperative the possible supply of a new strain of wheat that is resistant to a disease which recently swept the region.

In the meeting, the head of the cooperative told them about the problems which the relative unavailability of antiretroviral drugs cause locally in the face of a high HIV infection rate.

In a subsequent meeting with an official of M to discuss the approval of L's new wheat strain for import, the official suggests that L could pay for the necessary antiretroviral drugs and that this will be a very positive factor in the Government's consideration of the licence to import the new seed strain.

In a further meeting, the same official states that L should donate money to a certain charity suggested by the official which, the official assures, will then take the necessary steps to purchase and distribute the drugs.

Andre has raised concerns regarding potential bribery risks if L goes ahead with the suggestions made. However, the government official concerned has assured Andre that such payments comply with local laws and are standard custom and practice.

Required:

Advise the Directors of L plc, from the perspective of bribery risk.

39 IN-HOUSE CODE

The directors of John Groom Ltd, a small manufacturing company, have drafted an ethical code for use within the organisation, based on ones used by competitors and the industry trade organisation. The Board also plan to encourage suppliers to adopt the code.

Required:

Explain the legal status of this code.

40 NEW CODE

Matter

Cosby plc owns a small chain of supermarkets with an emphasis on organic, local produce. The Directors of Cosby plc are concerned that, despite having better quality produce than rivals, it is not competing as well as it would like against national supermarket chains.

The Marketing Director has proposed that Cosby plc should set up a new corporate code of ethics that could be used as part of its marketing effort. He is convinced that many customers will be influenced by such a code and has suggested that the following aspects could be incorporated:

1 All products should be purchased from local farms and suppliers where appropriate.

2 All packing materials should be obtained from renewable sources where feasible.

3 All suppliers to be paid on time.

4 All suppliers to be paid fair prices as determined by the Purchasing Manager.

Required:

Comment on EACH of the ethical values suggested by the Marketing Director, highlighting the benefit of each, together with any reservations you may have concerning them.

1	All products should be purchased from local farms and suppliers where appropriate.
2	All packing materials should be obtained from renewable sources where feasible.
3	All suppliers to be paid on time.
4	All suppliers to be paid fair prices as determined by the Purchasing Manager.

41 CHRIS

Chris, an AAT member, works for HJK and Co, a medium sized accountancy practice based in Manchester. Chris has performed accountancy and tax services for both Yin Ltd and Yang Ltd for many years.

Yin Ltd is currently in negotiations with the Board of Yang Ltd concerning a proposed takeover. Both Yin Ltd and Yang Ltd have requested that Chris help advise them.

Required:

(a) **Explain which TWO fundamental principles are threatened by the proposed takeover.**

> [blank answer box]

(b) Describe the ethical conflict resolution process Chris should undertake in deciding how to act in respect of this matter. Assume that he will be able to resolve the conflict of interest without needing to seek external professional advice.

> [blank answer box]

(c) Assuming he decides he can act for one of the clients, explain TWO issues Chris must consider when carrying out his work.

> [blank answer box]

42 SIMON

Simon, a member in practise, inherits from his Grandfather shares in a company that his firm audits.

Required:

(a) State which threat this situation represents.

> [blank answer box]

(b) Outline what Simon's best course of action is.

> [blank answer box]

43   LAST

Jason is an AAT member in practice. The following matter arose this week:

Matter

One evening Jason had a drink with an old friend, Brian, an AAT member currently working as an accountant for a large manufacturing company.

Brian was extremely worried about events in the company he works for. He had been asked by one of the directors to become involved in an arrangement that would lead to personal financial gain for the director at the expense of the company. Brian had been offered financial reward for this, and it had been made clear to him that he would lose his job if he didn't comply.

Required:

(a)   State which ethical principle Brian has already breached by talking about this situation?

```



```

(b)   Explain what course of action is most appropriate for Brian to take immediately.

```




```

(c)   If the situation cannot be resolved via internal action, explain what Brian should do.

```




```

44   SAFE AND SOUND

Lara is a professional accountant in practice. Detailed below are three matters that have arisen with respect to some of Lara's clients.

Matter A

The director of Company W, a listed company, sold a substantial shareholding prior to the announcement of worse than expected results for the company.

Matter B

Mike is CEO of Company X and is also a non-executive director of Company Y and sits on the remuneration committee of that company.

Graham is CEO of Company Y and is also a non-executive director of Company X and sits on the remuneration committee of that company.

Mike and Graham are good friends and play golf together every Saturday.

Matter C

The chairman of Company Z does not like conflict on the board.

When a new director is appointed, the chairman always ensures that the director's family members obtain highly paid jobs in the company and, in the case of children, that they are sponsored by Company Z through college.

Company Z is very profitable, although the board appears to be ineffective in querying the actions of the chairman.

Required:

For each of the situations above, identify the ethical threat to the client and recommend an ethical safeguard, explaining why that safeguard is appropriate.

Matter A

Matter B

Matter C

45 FREE HOLIDAYS

Sarah works for a firm of accountants called B & Sons LLP and has recently introduced a new client to the firm called Leigh Davis. She has also been appointed as the audit manager for the client's company A Tours Limited which specialises in luxury holidays in the Caribbean. Leigh Davis was keen for Sarah to be appointed the audit manager for his company as he has known Sarah for a long time. He has recently offered Sarah free holidays in the Caribbean in return for her not asking questions about some irregularities in his company's financial statements.

Required:

Analyse the above scenario from the perspective of the law relating bribery. In particular, explain which criminal offences the various parties have committed or are at risk of committing.

46   KEN

Ken is involved in illegal activities, from which he makes a considerable amount of money.

In order to conceal his gains from the illegal activities, he bought a bookshop intending to pass off his illegally gained money as profits from the legitimate bookshop business.

Ken employs Los to act as the manager of the bookshop and Mel as his accountant to produce false business accounts for the bookshop business.

Required:

(a)   **Explain what is meant by money laundering, the different categories of offence and possible punishments.**

(b) Analyse the above scenario from the perspective of the law relating to money laundering. In particular, explain which criminal offences may have been committed by the various parties.

AVBK, FAPR AND ETHICS

TASK 1.2

Assessment objective 2	Prepare accounting records and respond to errors, omissions and other concerns, in accordance with accounting and ethical principles and relevant regulations

TASK 1.3

Assessment objective 4	Apply ethical and accounting principles when preparing final accounts for different types of organisation, develop ethical courses of action and communicate relevant information effectively

TASK 1.5

Assessment objective 5	Prepare financial accounting information, comprising extended trial balances

47   BESS

Bess proves the accuracy of her sales and purchases ledgers by preparing monthly control accounts. At 1 September 20X7 the following balances existed in the business records, and the control accounts agreed.

	Debit £	Credit £
Sales ledger control account	188,360	2,140
Purchases ledger control account	120	89,410

The following are the totals of transactions which took place during September 20X7, as extracted from the business records.

	£
Credit sales	101,260
Credit purchases	68,420
Sales returns	9,160
Purchases returns	4,280
Cash received from customers	91,270
Cash paid to suppliers	71,840
Cash discounts allowed	1,430
Cash discounts received	880
Irrecoverable debts written off	460
Refunds to customers	300
Contra settlements	480

At 30 September 20X7 the balances in the sales and purchases ledgers, as extracted, totalled:

	Debit £	Credit £
Sales ledger balances	To be ascertained	3,360
Purchases ledger balances	90	To be ascertained

An initial attempt to balance the two ledgers showed that neither of them agreed.

The differences were found to be due to the following.

(i)   A contra settlement of £500 had not been included in the totals of transactions prepared for the control accounts.

(ii)   A new employee had mistakenly entered five copy sales invoices into the purchases day book as if they had been purchases invoices and entered the amounts to new purchases ledger accounts. The total of these invoices was £1,360.

(iii)   A £20 cash refund to a customer was made out of petty cash, and has not been included in the summary of transactions given above. The £20 was entered to the sales ledger as if it had been a cash receipt from the customer, and this resulted in a £40 credit balance on the account, which was still outstanding at 30 September 20X7.

When these errors had been corrected both control accounts agreed with the ledgers.

Prepare the sales ledger and purchases ledger control accounts for the month of September 20X7 after these errors had been corrected, and hence ascertain the missing totals of the ledger balances as indicated above.

48   SALLY

At 31 December 20X7 the totals of the subsidiary (sales) ledger balances of a sole trader were as follows.

£

Sales ledger control account   debit   384,600

After reviewing these balances in preparing the financial statements for the year ended 31 December 20X7, a number of adjustments are necessary.

(i)   A contra settlement had been agreed during the year offsetting an amount due from Sally Limited in the sales ledger of £1,080 against the balance due to that company in the purchases ledger. No entry had been made for this contra.

(ii)   The following debts due from sales ledger customers are to be written off.

Customer	£
P	840
Q	120
R	360
S	2,090
T	180

(iii)   The allowance for doubtful debts, which stood at £3,060 is to be increased to £5,200.

(iv)   During the year £200 cash received from AUT Limited had mistakenly been entered into the account of AUE Limited in the sales ledger.

Task

(a)   Prepare journal entries to give effect to adjustments (i) to (iv).

(b)   Calculate the amounts which should appear in the Statement of Financial Position as at 31 December 20X7 for receivables.

49   GEORGE

George has fixtures and fittings which were originally purchased on 1 May 20X0 for £8,400. These fixtures and fittings were sold on 1 December 20X1 for £6,000 having been depreciated at 15% straight line.

Task

(a)   What would be the carrying amount of the fixtures and fittings on the date of disposal if the depreciation is calculated on a monthly basis?

£

(b)   What would be the amount of profit or loss on disposal of the fixtures and fittings?

(Circle the correct answer for gain or loss)

Gain/Loss

£

50   NON-CURRENT ASSETS 1

NCA1 Limited is not registered for VAT and has a year end of 31 December 20X0.

The following is a purchase invoice received by NCA1 Limited:

Invoice # 212532		
To: NCA1 Limited 428 Hoole Road Chester CH4 GFV	Graham's Garages 32 Oldfield Way Chester CH12 RTH	**Date:** 28 November X0
		£
Vauxhall Van Delivery Tax Disc	Registration number ES54 DCS	15,000.00 250.00 210.00
Less part exchange Amount due Settlement terms: Strictly 60 days	Registration number FD01 VBA	(3,800.00) 11,660.00

The following information relates to the vehicle that was part exchanged:

Registration number	FD01 VBA
Length of ownership	4 years 2 months
Purchase price	£12,000.00

- Vehicles are depreciated at 30% on a reducing balance basis.

- Non-current assets are depreciated in the year of acquisition but not in the year of disposal.

You now need to complete the journal to reflect the purchase of the new van and the part exchange of the old van.

Narrative	Dr	Cr
Totals		

51 NON-CURRENT ASSETS 2

- Dave's Doors is a sole trader business that is registered for VAT at the standard rate of 20%. His year end is 31/12/X4.

- During 20X4, machine 'A' was sold, for total proceeds of £10,000 (cheque received).

- Machine 'A' was acquired on 01/07/X1 at a cost of £20,000 (excluding VAT).

- The depreciation policy for machinery is 10% per annum on a reducing balance basis. Non-current assets are depreciated in full in the year of acquisition but not in the year of disposal.

(a) What is the accumulated depreciation of machine 'A' in the year of disposal?

(b) Complete the journal to reflect the disposal of machine 'A'. A picklist of account names has been provided below. You are able to use an account name more than once. More rows than required have been provided below.

Narrative	Dr	Cr
Totals		

Picklist: Machinery at cost account, Machinery accumulated depreciation account, Disposals account, VAT Control, Bank (accounts can be used more than once)

(c) What was the profit or loss made on disposal?

---

52 MATTRESS

Daniel James is the proprietor of Mattress, a business which buys and sells bedroom furniture.

- The year end is 31 May 20X1.

- You are employed to assist with the book-keeping.

- The business currently operates a manual system consisting of a general ledger, a sales ledger and a purchases ledger.

- Double entry takes place in the general ledger. Individual accounts of receivables and payables are kept in memorandum accounts.

- You use a purchases day book, a sales day book, a purchases returns day book and a sales returns day book. Totals from the day books are transferred into the general ledger.

At the end of the financial year on 31 May 20X1, the balances were extracted from the general ledger and entered into an extended trial balance.

It was found that the total of the debit column of the trial balance did not agree with the total of the credit column. The difference was posted to a suspense account.

After the preparation of the extended trial balance the following errors were found:

(a) Motor expenses of £150 were debited to the Motor Vehicles at Cost account. Ignore depreciation.

(b) The VAT (sales tax) column in the purchases returns day book was undercast by £400.

(c) On 31 May 20X1 some of the fixtures and fittings were sold. The original cost of the assets was £11,000 and they were bought on 1 June 19W9. Depreciation provision to the date of disposal was made in the accounts and this totalled £4,400 for these fixtures and fittings. The disposal proceeds were £7,000. This money was correctly entered in the bank account, but no other entry was made.

(d) Sales of £9,500 were entered into the sales account as £5,900. All other entries were correct.

(e) A wages payment of £1,255 was debited to both the wages account and the bank account.

Task 1

Prepare journal entries to record the correction of the errors. Dates and narratives are not required.

Task 2

Showing clearly the individual debits and credits, update the suspense account using the journals from Task 1.

Suspense account

	£		£
		Balance b/d	13,510

53 YEAR-END 1

You are employed by Jane Parker who is a baker. You are her bookkeeper and she has asked you to create a trial balance. Below are the balances extracted from the main ledger at 30 April 20X2.

(a) Enter the balances into the columns of the trial balance provided below. Total the two columns and enter an appropriate suspense account balance to ensure that the two totals agree.

	£	Debit	Credit
Accruals	4,820		4,820
Prepayments	2,945	2,945	
Motor expenses	572	572	
Admin expenses	481	481	
Light and Heat	1,073	1073	
Revenue	48,729		48,729
Purchases	26,209	26209	
SLCA	5,407	5407	
PLCA	3,090		3090
Rent	45	45	
Purchase returns	306		306
Discounts allowed	567	567	
Capital	10,000		10,000
Loan	15,000		15,000
Interest paid	750	750	
Drawings	4,770	4770	
Motor vehicles – cost	19,000	19000	

Motor vehicle – accumulated depreciation	2,043		*7043*
VAT control owing	2,995		*2,995*
Wages	20,000	*20,000*	
Suspense account		*5,164*	
Totals		*86,987*	*86,983*

(b) Since the trial balance has been produced you have noticed a number of errors which are as follows:

(i) Jane put £5,000 into the business after receiving a large cheque as a Christmas present from her father. This has been put through the bank account but no other entries have been made.

(ii) The Gross column of the SDB has been overcast by £385.

(iii) The VAT column of the PDB has been undercast by £193.

(iv) An amount of £4,500 paid for rent has been credited to both the rent account and the bank account.

(v) An accrual for electricity at the year-end of £1,356 has been correctly credited to the accruals account but no other entry has been made.

Prepare the entries to correct these errors using the blank journal below. Dates and narratives are not required.

		Dr £	Cr
(i)	*Suspense*	*3000*	
	Capital		*3.000*
(ii)	*Suspense*	*385*	
	S.L.C.A		*385*
(iii)	*VAT*	*193*	
	Suspense		*193*
(iv)			
(v)			

54 ETB 1

You work for Highland Ltd, a company that makes and sells parts for vintage cars. You have been provided with an ETB that has been started by the current bookkeeper. However, she is now on holiday and the owner of Highland Ltd has asked that you create the adjustments and enter them onto the ETB to save time.

Make the appropriate entries in the adjustments column of the extended trial balance to take account of the following. The year-end date is 31 December 20X5.

(a) The allowances for doubtful debts figure is to be adjusted to 2% of receivables.

(b) A credit note received from a supplier for goods returned was mislaid. It has since been found and has not yet been accounted for. It was for £2,000 net plus £400 VAT.

(c) Rent is payable yearly in advance. For the 12 months to 31/10/X5 the rent is £12,000, the prepayment bought down has been included in the ledger balance. For the 12 months to 31/10/X6 the rent is £15,000.

(d) Inventory is valued at cost at £14,890. However, there was a leak in the storage cupboard and £3,000 worth of items has been damaged and need to be written off.

(e) The electricity bill of £450 for the 3 months ended 31 January 20X6 was received and paid in February 20X6.

Extended trial balance

Ledger account	Ledger balances		Adjustments	
	Dr £	Cr £	Dr £	Cr £
Accruals		1,330		300
Advertising	1,800			
Bank	7,912			
Capital		50,000		
Closing inventory			11,890	11,890
Depreciation charge				
Drawings	14,700			
Fixtures and fittings – accumulated depreciation		945		
Fixtures and fittings – cost	6,099			
Irrecoverable debts	345			
Allowance for doubtful debt adjustment				295
Electricity	1,587		300	
Loan	10,000			
Opening inventory	5,215			
Prepayment			12500	
Allowance for doubtful debts		485	295	
Purchases	78,921			
Purchase returns				2000
PLCA		14,000	2400	

	Dr	Cr		
Rent	25,000			*12500*
Revenue		145,825		
SLCA	9,500			
VAT control account		11,453		*400*
Wages	62,959			
	224,038	224,038	*27,385*	*27385*

55 ETB 2

You have the following extended trial balance. The adjustments have already been correctly entered. You now need to extend the figures into the statement of profit or loss and statement of financial position columns. Make the columns balance by entering figures and a label in the correct places.

Extended trial balance

Ledger account	Ledger balances		Adjustments		Statement of profit or loss		Statement of financial position	
	Dr £	Cr £	Dr £	Cr £	Dr £	Cr £	Dr £	Cr £
Accruals		2,300		425				*2725*
Advertising	1,800				*1800*			
Bank	7,912		1,175				*9087*	
Capital		40,000						*40,000*
Closing inventory			6,590	6,590		*6590*	*6540*	
Depreciation charge			821		*821*			
Drawings	14,700						*14700*	
Fixtures and fittings – accumulated depreciation		945		821				*1766*
Fixtures and fittings – cost	6,099						*6099*	
Interest	345				*345*			
Light and heat	1,587		706		*2293*			
Loan		10,000						*10,000*
Opening inventory	5,215				*5215*			
Prepayments	485		927	281			*1131*	
Purchases	75,921				*75921*			
PLCA		14,000						*14,000*
Rent and rates	38,000			927	*37073*			
Revenue		145,825				*145825*		

SLCA	9,500			1,175			*8.325*	
VAT control account		11,453						*11453*
Wages	62,959				*62959*			
							34,012 *34.01*	
	224,523	224,523	10,219	10,219	*186,427 186427*		*79344* *79944*	

56 INCOMPLETE 1

You are working on the accounts of Control Ltd for the year ended 30 September 20X6. You have the following information:

Sales for the year ended 30 September 20X6

- Credit sales amounted to £46,000 net of sales tax

- Cash sales amounted to £212,000 net of sales tax

- All sales are standard rated for sales tax at 20%.

Payments from the bank account for the year ended 30 September 20X6

- Payroll expenses £48,000
- Administration expenses £6,400 ignore sales tax
- Vehicle running costs £192,000 including sales tax at 20%
- Drawings £41,800
- Sales tax £17,300

Summary of balances available

Balance as at	30 September 20X5	30 September 20X6
Bank account	5,630	8,140
Trade receivables	4,120	5,710
Sales tax (credit balances)	4,200	4,575

(a) Calculate the figure for credit sales for entry into the receivables (sales ledger) control account?

£ *55,200*

(b) Using the figures given above (including your answer to part (a), prepare the sales ledger control account for the year ended 30 September 20X6, showing clearly the receipts paid into the bank as the balancing figure.

Receivables (Sales ledger) control account

Bal. b/d	*4,120*	*Bank paid*	*53,610*
Cr Sales	*55,200*	*Bal. c/d*	*5710*
	59,320		*59,310*

(c)   Calculate the cash sales inclusive of sales tax which have been paid into the bank account. All cash sales are banked.

(d)   Show a summarised bank account for the year ended 30 September 20X6.

Bank account

Handwritten: Bal b/d - 5630

Cash sales	254,400	Payroll	48,000
S.L.CA	53,610	Admin exp.	6400
		Veh run cost	192,000
		Drawing	41,800
		S. Tax	17,300
		bal. c/d.	8,140
			313,640

57   INCOMPLETE 2

You are given the following information about a sole trader called Brian as at 31 March 20X2:

The value of assets and liabilities were:

- Non-current assets at carrying amount   £14,000
- Bank   £2,500
- Trade payables   £10,300
- Opening capital (at 1 April 20X1)   £3,700
- Drawings for the year   £1,500

There were no other assets or liabilities.

Calculate the profit for the year ended 30 March 20X2.

£_____ *4,000*

58   INCOMPLETE 3

During the year ended 30 September 20X7, Elsie, a sole trader, made sales of £1,280,000 and made a sales margin of 25% on these. Rosemary made purchases of £970,200 during the year ended 30 September 20X7 and inventory was valued at £98,006 at the period end.

Using this information, complete the following:

(a)   Calculate the cost of goods sold for the year ended 30 September 20X7.

£_____

(b)   Calculate the value of the inventory at 1 October 20X6.

£_____

Handwritten: 960,000 c. of sales   320,000 G. prft

59   SOLE TRADER 1

You have the following trial balance for a sole trader known as Vincent Trading. All the necessary year-end adjustments have been made.

Vincent Trading has a policy of showing trade receivables net of any allowance for doubtful debts and showing trade payables and sundry payables as one total figure.

The statement of profit or loss for Vincent Trading shows a profit of £8,810 for the period.

Prepare a statement of financial position for the business for the year ended 30 June 20X8.

Vincent Trading		
Trial balance as at 30 June 20X8		
	Dr £	Cr £
Accruals		750
Bank		1,250
Capital		17,000
Closing inventory	7,850	7,850
Discounts received		900
Sundry payables		1,450
Purchase ledger control account		6,800
Depreciation charge	1,600	
Discounts allowed	345	
Allowance for doubtful debts adjustment	295	
Equipment accumulated depreciation		4,500
Wages	24,000	
Sales ledger control account	7,800	
Rent	5,250	
Revenue		164,000
Disposal		450
Prepayments	3,200	
Purchases	125,000	
Sales returns	1,500	
Opening inventory	3,450	
Equipment at cost	17,500	
Drawings	8,000	
General expenses	2,950	
Allowance for doubtful debts		840
VAT		2,950
	208,740	208,740

Vincent Trading

Statement of financial position as at 30 June 20X8

	£	£	£
Non-current assets	Cost	Depreciation	Carrying amount
Equipment at cost	17,500	4,500	13,000
Current assets			
S.L.C.A.		6,960	
Inventory		7,850	
P. payments		3,200	
Current liabilities		18,010	
P.L.C.A.	8,250		
Accrual	750		
Bank	1,250		
VAT	2,950		
		13,200	
Net current assets			4,810
Net assets			8,190
Financed by:			
Opening capital			17,000
Add: profit			8,810
Less: Drawings			8,000
Closing capital			17,810

60 SOLE TRADER 2

You are preparing the statement of financial position for Beale, a sole trader. All the necessary year-end adjustments have been made.

Beale has a policy of showing trade receivables net of any allowance for doubtful debts. The statement of profit or loss for Beale shows a loss of £4,350 for the period.

Prepare a statement of financial position for the business for the year ended 30 June 20X6.

Beale – Trial balance as at 30 June 20X6		
	Dr £	Cr £
Accruals		3,150
Administration expenses	45,000	
Bank		2,250
Capital		85,000
Cash	500	
Closing inventory	17,500	17,500
Depreciation charge	9,000	
Disposal of non-current asset		1,500
Motor vehicles at cost	45,000	
Motor vehicles accumulated depreciation		20,000
Opening inventory	15,000	
Allowance for doubtful debts		1,450
Allowance for doubtful debts adjustment	200	
Purchases	75,000	
Purchases ledger control account		23,750
Revenue		130,000
Sales ledger control account	68,550	
Selling expenses	9,150	
Drawings	3,200	
VAT		3,500
Total	288,100	288,100

Beale – Statement of financial position as at 30 June 20X6			
	£	£	£
Non-current assets	Cost	Depreciation	Carrying amount
Motor Veh. at cost	*45,000*	*20,000*	*25,000*
Current assets			
S.L.CA. (68,550 – 1450)		*67,100*	
Cash		*500*	
Closing inventory		*17,500*	
		85,100	
Current liabilities			
P.L.CA.	*23,750*		
Accruals	*3,150*		
Bank	*2,250*		
Vat	*3,500*		
		32,650	
Net current assets			*52,450*
Net assets			*77,450*
Financed by:			
Opening capital			*85,000*
Less:			*(4,350)*
Less: *Drawings*			*(3,200)*
Closing capital			*77,450*

61 PARTNER 1

You have the following information about a partnership business:

The financial year ends on 30 June.

- The partners are Gertrude, Eddie and Polonius.

- Partners' annual salaries

  - Gertrude   £18,000
  - Eddie   nil
  - Polonius   £36,000

- Partners' interest on capital

  - Gertrude   £2,000 per annum
  - Eddie   £2,000 per annum
  - Polonius   £2,000 per annum

- Partners' sales commission earned during the year
    - Gertrude   £8,250
    - Eddie   £6,800
    - Polonius   £4,715
- Profit share
    - Gertrude   40%
    - Eddie   40%
    - Polonius   20%

The statement of profit or loss for the partnership shows a profit for the year ended 30 June 20X9 of £220,000 before appropriations.

Prepare the appropriation account for the partnership for the year ended 30 June 20X9. Enter zeros where appropriate and use minus signs for deductions.

Partnership appropriation account for the year ended 30 June 20X9

	£
Profit for the year	
Salaries:	
Gertrude	
Eddie	
Polonius	
Interest on capital:	
Gertrude	
Eddie	
Polonius	
Sales commission:	
Gertrude	
Eddie	
Polonius	
Profit available for distribution	

Profit share:	
Gertrude	
Eddie	
Polonius	
Total residual profit distributed	

62 PARTNER 2

You have the following information about a partnership:

- The partners are Cordelia and Goneril, and the partnership produces luxury gifts for Fathers' Day and other special occasions.

- Regan joined the partnership on 1 May 20X7 when she introduced £128,000 into the business bank account.

- Profit share, effective until 30 April 20X7
    - Cordelia   35%   36750
    - Goneril   65%   68250

- Profit share, effective from 1 May 20X7
    - Cordelia   25%
    - Goneril   45%
    - Regan   30%

- Goodwill was valued at £105,000 on 30 April 20X7.

- Goodwill is to be introduced into the partners' capital accounts on 30 April and then eliminated on 1 May.

(a) **Show the entries required to introduce the goodwill into the partnership accounting records.**

Account name	Dr	Cr

Cordelia is thinking of leaving the partnership next year. It is estimated that Regan's good reputation will have added £22,000 to the goodwill value by then.

(b) **Calculate the goodwill to be introduced into Cordelia's capital account at the time of her departure.**

63 PARTNER 3

Macbeth, Hamlet and Will are in partnership selling cases for mobile phones.

- Will retired from the partnership on 30 June 20X5. He has agreed that the partnership will pay what he is due from the bank account in full.

- Profit share, effective until 30 June 20X5
    - Macbeth   30%
    - Hamlet   40%
    - Will   30%

- Profit share, effective from 1 July 20X5
    - Macbeth   50%
    - Hamlet   50%

- Goodwill was valued at £50,000 on 30 June 20X5.

- Goodwill is to be introduced into the partners' capital accounts on 30 June and then eliminated on 1 July.

- At the 30 June 20X5 the partners had the following balances on their capital and current accounts:

    - Macbeth £7,000 (capital a/c) and £11,000 (current a/c)

    - Hamlet £8,000 (capital a/c) and £9,000 (current a/c)

    - Will £9,000 (capital a/c) and £7,000 (current a/c)

Prepare the capital account for Will, showing clearly the transfer from the current account and the amount paid to Will on his retirement.

Capital account – Will

		Balance b/d	9,000

64 INTEGRITY

Frankie is an AAT member working for Lightfoots Ltd as an assistant to the management accountant. His finance director has asked him to post a journal to transfer £20,000, a material sum, out of maintenance costs and into non-current assets, thus boosting profit for the period. Frankie has checked the details and feels that there is no justification for the journal.

Required:

Explain what Frankie should do, highlighting both internal and external courses of action.

65 SUSTENANCE

At a recent Board meeting of Sustenance plc the topic of sustainability arose. The main view given was that attempts to incorporate sustainability would inevitably increase costs and reduce profits. When the Finance Director tried to explain that this was not the case, the Marketing Director commented that sustainability was nothing to do with accountants anyway.

Required:

(a)   Outline the roles of professional accountants in contributing to sustainability.

(b)   Describe three ways in which an increased emphasis on sustainability can result in improved profits for a firm.

66   TIO RINO

Tio Rino is a global mining company that has received much criticism in the past over its sustainability record. Press coverage has focussed on environmental damage, pollution, labour and human rights abuses and deforestation as well as criticism that Tio Rino mines coal (which contributes to global warming when burnt) and uranium (which contributes to concerns over nuclear power).

However, on its website the firm states the following:

'Our business is sustainably finding, mining and processing mineral resources.'

Required:

FOR EACH of the Triple Bottom Line reporting headings suggest TWO ways that a mining company such as Tio Rino can be a sustainable mining company.

People

Profit

Planet

67 HOGGS FURNITURE

Jacob is a professional accountant working for Hoggs Furniture Ltd ('Hoggs'), a furniture manufacturer that supplies many high street retailers.

Matter

At the last management meeting it was announced that a major client of the company was threatening to terminate their contract with Hoggs unless it could demonstrate a clear commitment to sustainability. The team were unclear what this meant for Hoggs and asked Jacob to investigate further.

Required:

(a)   **Explain what is meant by 'sustainability'.**

(b)   **Explain FOUR areas that Jacob should appraise in order to answer the client's concerns.**

(c)   **List THREE other ways Jacob can contribute to sustainability as an accountant.**

68   STEVEN

As financial controller Steven has been asked to sign off N&Q Ltd's year-end accounts. He joined the company only three months ago.

The accounts include a note that is incorrect. Having investigated the matter, Steven recognises that this is a genuine mistake and not a deliberate attempt to mislead.

The Managing Director does not want to produce new accounts because of its inherent cost, but Steven does not feel it appropriate that he signs off something that has an error in it.

What action should Steven take?

69   FINANCE

'Ultimate DPF' is a sole trader who makes exhaust systems for diesel-powered cars. Jenny Green, the owner and founder of the business, is looking at expanding operations and is considering different ways of raising the additional finance required.

Option 1

The first approach Jenny is considering is finding new business partners to come into the business with her but is unsure about whether to set up the business as a partnership or a limited company.

Explain to Jenny THREE differences between partnerships and limited companies (excluding those relating to raising finance) and TWO implications this choice will make on raising the finance required.

Difference 1
Difference 2
Difference 3
Implication for finance 1
Implication for finance 2

Option 2

The second approach Jenny is considering is to try to raise a bank loan and read online that banks like to look at the Statement of Financial Position (SOFP) when assessing a loan application. This confused Jenny as she thought the SOFP was produced primarily for shareholders.

Explain THREE elements of a SOFP that a bank would be interested in and why

Aspect of SOFP	Reason why the bank would look at this
1	
2	
3	

List THREE stakeholders (other than a bank) who would use a SOFP and explain why

Stakeholder	Why they would use the SOFP
1	
2	
3	

70 ACCOUNTING FUNDAMENTALS

(1) Describe and explain what the accounting equation is, its importance and how it is used.

(2)   Describe and explain what the Statement of Profit and Loss is, its importance and how it is used.

(3)   Describe and explain what the Statement of Financial Position is, its importance and how it is used.

(4)   Compare the Statement of Profit and Loss and the Statement of Financial position by explaining the similarities/differences between the two, and the advantages and disadvantages of each.

71   CASH

Explain THREE reasons why the net profit of a business for a period is not necessarily the same as the net cash generated in the same period. Give TWO examples for each reason.

Reason 1
Reason 2
Reason 3

72   CYCLE

Mthbe is a professional accountant with his own small practice. He performs accountancy and tax services for a wide range of small clients including many sole traders.

Required:

(a)   **Explain, with justification, TWO areas in which Mthbe needs to keep his technical knowledge up-to-date.**

Area 1
Area 2

(b)   **According to the AAT CPD policy how often should Mthbe complete a CPD Cycle?**

(c)   **List the recommended stages in the AAT's CPD cycle.**

73   SARAH

Sarah is an AAT member working for a small accountancy practice. She has received a call from a property agent asking for the following information about a client.

- Accounts for the previous three years.

- An assurance that they will be able to meet the rent for a proposed property rental.

Required:

(a)   **Advise Sarah on the appropriate course of action, with regards to giving the agent the Accounts for the previous three years.**

(b)   **Advise Sarah on the appropriate course of action, with regards to giving the agent an assurance the client will be able to pay.**

74 ADAM

Adam, an AAT member within the UK, works for a firm of accountants, LOFT and Co, with a range of clients.

Matter 1

Adam has found an error in a client's tax affairs. The client has refused to disclose this known error, even after Adam has given notice of this error and an appropriate amount of time has been allowed to take action.

Required:

State to whom Adam is obliged to report this refusal to and the information surrounding it.

Matter 2

LOFT and Co recently billed a client, H Ltd, £5,000 and were very surprised when they received a cheque for £50,000 in settlement of the invoice.

The Finance Director of H Ltd explained that it was a mistake on his part but asked whether LOFT and Co could send a cheque for the overpayment of £45,000 to Q Ltd, a different company and not one of LOFT's clients.

Required:

Discuss whether or not LOFT and Co should agree to the payment.

MMAC

TASK 1.5

Assessment objective 4	Use relevant spreadsheet skills to analyse, interpret and report management accounting data

75 ALLOCATION AND APPORTION

An organisation has three departments Mending, Stores and Canteen.

The budgeted overhead costs for the organisation are as follows:

	£
Rent	30,000
Building maintenance costs	45,000
Machinery insurance	2,400
Machinery depreciation	11,000
Machinery running cost	6,000
Power	7,000

There are specific costs that are to be allocated to each cost centre as follows:

	£
Mending	4,000
Stores	1,000
Canteen	2,000

The following information about the various cost centres is also available:

	Mending	Stores	Canteen	Total
Floor space (m²)	8,000	5,000	2,000	15,000
Power usage %	80	10	10	100
Value of machinery (£000)	140	110	–	250
Machinery hours (000)	50	30	–	80
Value of equipment (£000)	15	5	–	20

Allocate and apportion the costs to the three departments.

Overhead cost	Basis	Mending £	Stores £	Canteen £	Total £
Specific overheads	Allocate	9,000	1,000	2,000	12,000
Rent	floor space	16,000	10,000	4,000	32,000
Building maintenance	floor space	24,000	15,000	6,000	5,000
Machinery insurance	Value of m/c	1344	1056	–	2,400
Machinery depreciation	Value of equip.	6160	4840	–	11,000
Machinery running cost	mach. hours	3750	2250	–	6,000
Power	Power usage	5600	700	700	7,000
Total		60854	34,846	12,700	75,400

76 REAPPORTIONMENT

An organisation has three departments Mending, Stores and Canteen.

The budgeted overhead allocated and apportioned into each department are as follows:

	£
Mending	60,854
Stores	34,846
Canteen	12,700

The following information about the various cost centres is also available:

	Mending	Stores	Canteen
Number of employees	15	5	2
Value of stores requisitions (£000)	50	–	–

Reapportion the costs to the production department.

Overhead cost	Basis	Mending £	Stores £	Canteen £	Total £
Sub-Total		60,854	34,846	12,700	108,400
Re-apportion Canteen		9525	3,175	(12,700)	
Re-apportion Stores					
Total					

77 PACKAGING

Packaging Ltd has the following original budget and actual performance for product RB for the year ending 31 July.

	Budget	Actual
Volume sold	180,000	259,200
	£000	£000
Sales revenue	3,600	6,480
Less costs:		
Direct materials	630	954
Direct labour	720	864
Overheads	1,764	2,210
Operating profit	486	2,452

Both direct materials and direct labour are variable costs, but the overheads are fixed.

Complete the table below to show a flexed budget and the resulting variances against this budget for the year. Round to the nearest £1,000.

Show the actual variance amount, for sales and each cost, in the column headed 'Variance' and indicate whether this is Favourable or Adverse by entering F or A in the final column. If neither F nor A enter 0.

	Flexed Budget	Actual	Variance	Favourable F or Adverse A
Volume sold	259,200	259,200		
	£000	£000	£000	
Sales revenue	5184	6,480	1296	F
Less costs:				
Direct materials	907	954	47	A
Direct labour	1037	864	173	F
Overheads	1764	2,210	446	A
Operating profit	1476	2,452	976	F

78   LF

LF Ltd manufactures three products – X, Y and Z – that use the same machines.

The budgeted statements of profit or loss for the three products are as follows:

	Z	X	Y
	£000	£000	£000
Sales	1,000	1,125	625
Prime costs	(500)	(562.50)	(437.50)
Variable overheads	(250)	(187.50)	(62.50)
Fixed overheads	(200)	(315)	(130)
Profit/(loss)	50	60	(5)
Annual sales demand (units)	5,000	7,500	2,500
Machine hours per unit	20	21	26

Fixed overheads are absorbed on the basis of machine hours. The budgeted machine hours based on normal capacity were 322,500 hours.

However, after the budget had been formulated, an unforeseen condition has meant that during the next period the available machine capacity has been limited to 296,500 hours.

Task 1

Determine the order of priority (rankings) of production of the three products.

Task 2

Determine the optimum production plan for the next period.

Task 3

Determine the total profit resulting from the production plan in Task 2.

79   HEATH

Heath Ltd makes a product 'H' which has a selling price of £19 per unit with a total variable cost of £12 per unit. Heath Ltd estimates that the fixed costs associated with this product are £17,150.

(a)   Calculate the budgeted breakeven, in units, for product H.

(b)   Calculate the budgeted breakeven, in £s, for product H.

(c)   Complete the table below to show the budgeted margin of safety in units and the margin of safety percentage if Heath Ltd sells 4,000 units or 5,000 units of product H.

Units of H sold	4,000	5,000
Margin of safety (units)		
Margin of safety percentage (2dp)		

(d)   If Heath Ltd wishes to make a profit of £24,850, how many units of H must it sell?

(e)   If Heath Ltd increases the selling price of H by £2 what will be the impact on the breakeven point and the margin of safety assuming no change in the number of units sold?

A   The breakeven point will decrease and the margin of safety will stay the same

B   The breakeven point will decrease and the margin of safety will increase

C   The breakeven point will stay the same but the margin of safety will decrease

D   The breakeven point will increase and the margin of safety will decrease

80   BLINDS

One of the machines in the Finishing department is nearing the end of its useful life and Blinds Ltd is considering purchasing a replacement machine.

Estimates have been made for the initial capital cost, sales income and operating costs of the replacement machine, which is expected to have a useful life of three years:

	Year 0 £000	Year 1 £000	Year 2 £000	Year 3 £000
Capital expenditure	547			
Other cash flows:				
Sales income		290	340	400
Operating costs		120	120	120

The company appraises capital investment projects using a 10% cost of capital.

(a)   Complete the table below and calculate the net present value of the proposed replacement machine (to the nearest £000).

	Year 0 £000	Year 1 £000	Year 2 £000	Year 3 £000
Capital expenditure	-547			
Sales income		290	340	400
Operating costs		(120)	(120)	(120)
Net cash flows		170	220	280
PV factors	1.0000	0.909	0.826	0.751
Discounted cash flows	-547	155	182	210
Net present value	0			

(b) Calculate the payback period.

(c) If the NPV of a project is nil then the cost of capital equals the Internal Rate of Return (IRR)

True or false?

(d) If the IRR of an investment is higher than the companies cost of capital then the investment should go ahead.

True or false?

EXAM – PART II – PRACTICE TASKS

The excel files required for the tasks in the scenarios can be found on MyKaplan account in AVSY Exam Kit: Scenarios Excel Data & Answers.

Please go to www.mykaplan.co.uk and login to the AVSY section.

SCENARIO 1

SLICK PARTZ

You are an Accounting Technician working for the UK Branch of a company called **Slick Partz**. Your branch is a franchise of the parent company which is based in Europe. Slick Partz manufactures parts for hospital equipment at its factory in main land Europe and these are then sold to franchisees. The franchise is then responsible for selling the parts to hospitals in its sales area.

The franchise buys the parts from the parent company in Euros (€) but sells to the hospitals in GB Pounds (£).

The excel workbook can be found on MyKaplan in Exam Preparation, AVSY Exam Kit: Scenarios Excel Data & Answers.

Required:

TASK 1

(a)   Download and save the Excel file **Slick Partz**.

(b)   In Column E insert a formula to convert the Euro cost price into £ cost price.   The conversion rate is £1:€0.84.

(c)   In Column F insert a formula that adds a 20% mark-up on the cost.

(d)   Format column D to currency € Euros to 2 decimal places and columns E and F to currency £ to 2 decimal places.

(e)   Copy the 'Data Import' worksheet into the Subtotals worksheet.

(f)   Set the page orientation to portrait and fit the data to the width of one page.

TASK 2

(a)   Sort the data in the 'Subtotals' worksheet in preparation for carrying out subtotalling. The subtotals that are needed are for Model and Salesperson.

(b)   Create subtotals for Model, summing the Sales quantity.

(c)   Create a further subtotal for Salesperson, summing the Sales quantity.

(d)   Convert the worksheet to show formulas.

(e)   Set the page orientation to landscape.

TASK 3

(a)   In 'Data Import' worksheet and Auto-Filter the data.

(b)   Filter by sales operative 'Monty Video'.

(c)   Copy the result and paste it into Cell A1 in the 'Profit Calculation' worksheet.

(d)   Return to the 'Data Import' worksheet and remove the 'Monty Video' filter.

(e)   In Cells J1, K1 and L1 create 3 new headings of 'Total Cost', 'Total Revenue' and 'Profit'. Use the same format as on earlier headings.

(f)   In Column J use a formula to calculate the total revenue in £

(g)   In Column K use a formula to calculate the cost of sales in £

(h)   In Column L use a formula to calculate the profit in £

(i)   In Cell L26 create a formula that calculates the average profit. Create a suitable heading in K26.

(j)   In Cell L27 create a formula that calculates the largest amount of profit. Create a suitable heading in K27.

(k)   In Cell L28 create a formula that calculates the smallest amount of profit. Create a suitable heading in K28.

(l)   Format the values to currency £ to 2 decimal places.

TASK 4

(a)   Open the Data Import worksheet.

(b)   Using the data create a Pivot Table in a new worksheet that shows the sales quantity of each individual model sold by each salesperson.

(c)   Rename the worksheet 'Pivot' and move it to the right of the Profit Calculation sheet.

(d)   Create a Pivot Chart and locate it on the Pivot worksheet. The type of chart should be a Clustered Column Chart. Add a suitable title to the chart.

(e)   Add Customer as a Filter and select CUS1.

TASK 5

(a)   Open the 'Product Lookup' worksheet.

(b)   In cell A2 type "Product Code", font size 12 and bold. In cell B2 create a list of product codes from the data import worksheet using Data Validation.

(c)   In cell A6 type "Cost Price", font size 12 and bold. Format cell B6 to have a border, grey fill, bold size 12 font and currency £ to 2 decimal places.

(d)   In cell A9 type "Stock quantity", font size 12 and bold. Format Cells B9 and B12 to have a border, a grey fill and bold size 12 font.

(e)   In cell B6 create a VLOOKUP to look up the Product Code chosen in Cell B2 in the Data Import worksheet and return the Cost Price. The VLOOKUP should be set to look for only exact matches.

(f)   In cell B9 create a VLOOKUP to look up the Product-Code chosen in Cell B2 in the Data Import worksheet and return the Stock Quantity. The VLOOKUP should be set to look for only exact matches.

(g)   In Cell B12, use an IF statement that produces the word "Re-order" if the value in Cell B9 is greater than 0 and less than 20 **and** remains blank if the value is greater than 20.

SCENARIO 2

BETTABAKE

You work for a small bakery. They are very good at making cakes but not very good at doing their budgets. They are constantly running out of material because they do not predict accurately what cakes they are going to make that day.

The company makes four different cakes.

The Whirl

Splash

Butterbun

Chocco

Ingredient requirements for each product are:

Cake	Eggs	Flour	Sugar	Butter	Cream
The Whirl	1	50g	35g	28g	12g
Splash	1.5	30g	18g	22g	10g
Butterbun	2	65g	27g	24g	0
Chocco	1	55g	30g	21g	0

The following information is also available with regards to costs:

Ingredient	Quantity	Total cost
Eggs	12	£1.50
Flour	200g	£1.80
Sugar	200g	£2.20
Butter	1000g	£6.00
Cream	300g	£2.50

Required:

The Production Manager wants you to prepare a spreadsheet workbook that will help her with her budgets.

TASK 1

Download and save the workbook called **Bettabake**.

(a)   On the Budget data worksheet use a formula in column D to calculate the cost per ingredient i.e. per egg or per gram.

(b)   On the 'Cost per cake' worksheet use the 'Ingredients' worksheet to create formulas in cells B2 to F5 that will calculate the total cost of each ingredient for each cake. Give consideration to where absolute and relative referencing will be required.

(c)   Add a column for 'Total Cost per Cake'.

(d)   Format all cells as currency £ to 2 decimal places.

TASK 2

(a)   On the 'Budget' worksheet insert the following quantities in column B:

The Whirl   30

Splash   9

Butterbun   15

Chocco   24

(b)   In the cells C2:G5 create a formula that calculates the quantity of ingredients required to manufacture the volume of cakes entered in Column B. Use absolute referencing where necessary.

(c)   In row 6 use a function to calculate the totals.

(d)   In row 7 use the following information to calculate the purchase quantities for each ingredient.

Eggs are purchased in boxes of 360.

All other ingredients are purchased by the kg (1000g).

(e)   Add a formula to row 7 that will round the purchase quantity up to the nearest whole box or kg.

TASK 3

The current selling prices for each cake are:

Cake	£
The Whirl	0.90
Splash	1.20
Butterbun	1.10
Chocco	1.50

(a)   Insert the selling price data for each cake from the list above in cells C14:C17

(b)   Use a VLOOKUP to look up the cost price from the 'Cost per Cake' worksheet in cells B14 to B17

(c)   Use a formula in cells D14 to D17 to calculate profit

(d)   In cells E14:E17 use a formula to calculate the total profit and the total profit in cell E18

TASK 4

(a)   Your manager informs you that the fixed costs are £250. He would like to know how many Splash cakes need to be sold to break even. Use What if analysis to determine the number of Splash cakes required.

(b)   **BEFORE** you click OK take a screen shot of the What-if analysis and paste it into a new worksheet. Name the worksheet 'Screenshot'.

(c)   Return to the Budget worksheet and round the number of Splash cakes in column B to ensure Bettabake will break even.

TASK 5

(a) Your manager wants to calculate the future possible sales amounts for The Whirl. On the 'Whirl' worksheet produce a scatter graph with a line of best fit showing the trend on the sales.

(b) Use the Forecast function to predict the sales for weeks 11 and 12. Round the answers down to the nearest whole cake.

SCENARIO 3

CRAZY CARS

You work as a payroll assistant for a car sales company called Crazy Cars.

Basic wage

The basic wage is dependent on the number of full years each employee has worked for the business.

An employee's starting rate (for the first 12 months) is £160 per week.

The basic rate per week increases by 10% for each full year of employment up to a maximum of 5 years.

Commission earned

Each employee receives 5% of the profit they have earned from each car they have sold that week.

If a car is sold at a loss, then 5% of this loss is deducted from the employee's commission.

Any cars sold at a loss must be highlighted for the Finance Manager.

Weekly bonus

Any member of staff who earns more than the average commission each week receives an extra £100 bonus.

Required:

TASK 1

Download and save the file **Crazy Cars**.

(a) In Cell B10 use a function that will show todays date.

(b) In column C calculate the number of days each employee has worked for Crazy Cars with reference to the function in Cell B10. Ensure the format of these cells shows the number of days rather than the date.

(c) In column D convert the number of days into years (assume 365 days in a year).

(d) In column E use a formula to round the number of years down to the nearest year.

TASK 2

On the 'Basic Pay' worksheet:

(a) Create a table, starting in Cell A1, that's shows the number of years employed (up to 15 years) and the weekly wage amount. Make sure the table has suitable headings and use a formula for calculating the change in the weekly pay.

(b) Format the basic wage to pounds and pence.

(c) Add a border around each cell.

TASK 3

On the 'Car Sales Information' worksheet:

(a) Import the 'Car Sales' text file found on MyKaplan in Exam Preparation, AVSY Exam Kit: Scenarios Excel Data & Answers into Sheet 1/cell $A$1. The text file will need to be downloaded and saved before starting the task. Re-name the sheet 'Car Sales Information'.

(b) In column E create use a formula to calculate the profit made for each vehicle.

(c) Use conditional formatting in column E to identify any vehicles that have been sold at a loss. Have the cell turn red with black text.

(d) In column F use an IF statement to calculate the amount of commission earned on each vehicle. The cell should show the amount of commission earnt but if a loss is made then the cell should be blank.

(e) All monetary values should be formatted to currency (£) to 2 decimal places.

TASK 4

Using the 'Car Sales Information' worksheet:

(a) Create a pivot table in a new worksheet that shows the commission earned by each employee per make of car.

(b) Format the values in the Pivot table as currency £ to 2 decimal places.

(c) Name the Pivot Table worksheet as 'Pivot'.

(d) Move the Pivot Table worksheet to the right of the Car Sales Information worksheet.

TASK 5

On the 'Total Pay' worksheet:

(a) In Column B use a VLOOKUP from the 'Employee Information' tab to extract the number of years each employee has been employed.

(b) In Column C use a VLOOKUP from the Basic Pay worksheet to calculate the applicable basic weekly pay for each employee.

(c) In Column D use a VLOOKUP from the Pivot table worksheet to enter the Commission earned per employee.

(d) In cell D10 use a function to show the average commission earned, add a suitable title in cell C10.

(e)   In Column E use an IF statement to calculate the bonus.

(f)   In Column F use a formula to calculate the total pay for each employee for the week and the total wages the company are paying that week.

(g)   Format all monetary amounts to pounds and pence.

TASK 6

The Finance Director wants to see how each sales person has contributed to the total commission earned.

(a)   Create a pie chart using the 'Total Pay' worksheet to show each employees commission as a proportion of the total commission.

(b)   Give the pie chart a suitable title and apply percentage labels to the chart.

(c)   Save this on a new worksheet called 'Pie Chart' and move the sheet to the right of the Total Pay worksheet.

SCENARIO 4

GOODTIME TRAVEL

Goodtime Travel is a firm of Travel Agents that specialises in long haul package holidays. They buy the flights and hotel rooms in bulk from the airlines and hotels. They are a reputable firm and get most of their custom from customers who have used their service before.

They have recently invested in a marketing campaign to try and encourage new customers to use their service. The Marketing Manager has said that the campaign will be viewed as a success if at least 40% of income each week is generated from new customers.

Repeat customers

Customers can receive discounts off their holidays. A discount will only be given if a customer has booked a previous holiday with Goodtime Travel. A discount is given of 2p per mile flown on the previous holiday.

This discount is then deducted from the price of the current holiday. However, the Finance Director is considering adapting the discount rates so that they are different for each destination. Details of the miles travelled for each destination are:

Required:

TASK 1

Download and save the excel file **Goodtime Travel**.

On the 'Discounts' worksheet:

(a)   In Cell E1 enter the discount rate given in the scenario and give it a suitable heading in D1.

(b)   In Column C create a formula to calculate the discount for a particular destination.

(c)   Format the discount column as currency (£) to 2 decimal places.

TASK 2

On the 'Weekly Sales' worksheet:

(a)   Create a Discount column in column F. Use a VLOOKUP from the 'Discounts' worksheet to calculate any applicable discounts.

(b)   Format currency to 2 decimal places in £.

(c)   In the column G, use a formula to calculate the amount owing for each booking deducting any discounts for repeat customers.

TASK 3

(a)   Create a pivot table in a new worksheet to show how much revenue has been generated from new customers compared to existing customers for the different destinations.

(b)   Call this worksheet 'Pivot' and move it to the right of the 'Weekly sales' worksheet.

(c)   In cell K9 on the Pivot sheet create an expression to calculate the total % of income generated from new customers.

(d)   In cell K10 use an IF function – based on the outcome of task 3c – for the Marketing Director to determine whether the campaign was a success. 'Successful' should appear if more than 40% of the income is generated from new customers and 'Unsuccessful' if less than 40% of the income is generated from new customers. Format the outcome of the IF formula by making it bold, and enlarging the text to font size 16.

TASK 4

The Finance Director is considering changing the discount on offer per mile for repeat customers. He wants the discounts amounts for the following destinations changed to:

Destination	New Discount	Currently
Sydney	£250.00	£424.00
Fiji	£300.00	£404.36

On the What If Analysis worksheet:

(a)   Copy all the Discount information from the discount worksheet into the What IF Analysis worksheet.

(b)   Using What If Analysis – Goal Seek, calculate what the revised discount rate per mile needs to be to reduce the discount offered for Sydney. Copy and 'paste–special values' the result to cell D20. Provide a suitable heading in A20. Reset the original discount rate per mile to 2p.

(c)   Using What If Analysis – Goal Seek, calculate what the revised discount rate per mile needs to be to reduce the discount offered for Fiji. Copy and 'paste–special values' the result to cell D22. Provide a suitable heading in A22. Reset the original discount rate per mile to 2p.

SCENARIO 5

STAR TICKETS

THE CITY OF
LIVERPOOL COLLEGE
LRC

You work for Star Tickets, a small company selling tickets to music concerts.

Star Tickets buys tickets from concert venues to sell them on to customers. The face value of the tickets is £50, but Star Tickets receives discounts depending on which day the concert takes place. Star Tickets sales staff aim to sell each ticket for as much as possible; if they sell a ticket for more than its purchase price they receive a bonus. The discount percentages are:

Monday – Wednesday 25%

Thursday 10%

Friday–Sunday no discount is offered

Customers can pay in instalments, although management have said that at the end of each day the total outstanding balance owed by all customers cannot be greater than 10% of the total sales generated that day.

Management are also keen to identify any unpopular artists whose tickets are not making a profit for the company.

Star Tickets have asked you to help them create a spreadsheet to help manage their ticket sales. They have given you the details for today's sales:

Artist	Day of concert	Customer payment		Ticket seller
		Sales price	Amount paid	
Nancy Arbuckle	Saturday	£30	£10	Jane
Other Way	Tuesday	£60	£60	Mark
Down Stream	Wednesday	£90	£90	Mark
Upright Legs	Friday	£80	£80	Karen
Other Way	Tuesday	£30	£15	Jane
Nancy Arbuckle	Saturday	£45	£45	Mark
Down Stream	Friday	£34	£34	Jane

Required:

TASK 1

(a) Download and save the excel workbook called **Star Tickets**.

(b) On the 'Data' worksheet use formulas to calculate the discounted price in column D.

(c) On the 'Data' worksheet produce 3 lists in columns F, G and H. Column F is for the Artists, column G is for the days of the week and column H is for the ticket sellers.

TASK 2

(a) On the 'Ticket Sales' worksheet using the 'Data' worksheet create drop down lists for Artist, Day of Week and Ticket Seller in columns A, B and C respectively. The drop down list will need to be available for 7 rows.

(b) In the 'Purchase Price' column, create a VLOOKUP that selects the correct discounted purchase price based on the day of the week.

(c) Enter the data from the scenario for the 'Sales price' and 'Amount paid'.

(d)   In the 'Amount Outstanding' column create a formula that calculates what is outstanding.

(e)   In the 'Profit/Loss' column create a formula that calculates the profit or a loss.

(f)   In the 'Bonus Payable?' column, create an 'IF' function to determine whether a bonus is due. If a bonus is due the function should return Yes if not then the function should return No.

(g)   Set all monetary amounts on each worksheet to currency £ and 2 decimal places.

TASK 3

(a)   On the 'Ticket Sales' worksheet use conditional formatting to fill cells red in the 'Profit/loss' column where a loss has been made.

(b)   Label Row 10 'Totals'. Create totals below the 'Sales Price' and the 'Amount Outstanding' column. Use single line border at the top of these cells and double line border at the bottom of the cells.

(c)   In Cell G15 create a formula to determine how much of the sales are outstanding as a percentage of total sales made. Provide a suitable bold heading in cell F15 and right align the heading.

(d)   In cell H15 create an IF Function that determines whether the percentage would be acceptable to management. The function should return either 'OK' or 'Not Acceptable'.

TASK 4

(a)   Create a pivot table in a new worksheet to show how much profit each ticket seller has made, by Artist.

(b)   Rename the worksheet 'Pivot' and move it to the right of the 'Ticket Sales' worksheet.

(c)   Use conditional formatting to highlight the cells yellow in the pivot table where a loss has been made.

SCENARIO 6

DEPRECIATION

A business buys a motor van for £20,000 and depreciates it at 10% per annum by the diminishing balance method.

Download the **Depreciation** file and using simple formula calculate:

(a)   The depreciation charge for the first and second year of the motor van's use.

(b)   Calculate the carrying value at the end of the each year.

(c)   Complete the Statement of financial position extract.

(d)   Format all values with the thousand separator and zero decimal places.

SCENARIO 7

MARK-UP AND MARGIN

The aim of this task is to create a spreadsheet that will enable a user to be able to calculate sales, cost of sales or profit based on a mark-up or margin.

Download the **Mark-up and margins** file.

(a) Insert formulas into the coloured cells to enable the user to calculate:

   (i)   cost of sales and profit from a sales figure of £1,200

   (ii)   sales and profit from a cost of sales figure of £60

   (iii) sales and cost of sales from a profit figure of £80.

          The formulas should work if the mark-up or margin figure changes and if the sales, cost of sales or profit figure is updated.

(b) Format the numbers in Currency format, to two decimal places with a 1000 separator comma.

SCENARIO 8

VARIANCES

Victor Ltd is comparing its budget for the quarter with the actual revenue and costs incurred. Victor has planned to make and sell 1,000 units but has actually made and sold 1,400 units.

(a) Download the **Variance** file.

(b) Open the Original budget worksheet and in cell H1 calculate the percentage to flex the budget in line with the information above.

(c) In cell C3 enter the title 'Flexed Budget'. Calculate the flexed budget for the relevant entries using absolute referencing where appropriate.

(d) In cell D3 enter the title 'Actual Results'. The actual revenue and costs are shown in the worksheet headed 'Actual Results'. Use copy and 'paste link' to insert these from the source worksheet into column D of the 'Original Budget' worksheet.

(e) In cell E3 insert the title 'Variance'. Calculate the variance for the revenue and each cost. Show these in column F.

(f) In cell A10 insert the title 'Operating profit'. Calculate the operating profit for the original, flexed budget and actual results.

(g) Calculate the overall variance in cell E10.

(h) Use conditional formatting in column E to show all the favourable variances in green and adverse variances in red.

(i) Format all values with the thousand separator and to zero decimal place. Font to Calibri size 12, bold headings to the table, autofit all cells.

(j) Copy the range A3:D10, and paste only the values into a new worksheet. Name this worksheet Contribution. Insert a new row in an appropriate place in the table to be able to calculate the budgeted contribution, flexed contribution, actual contribution and the variance.

(k) Calculate the breakeven point in units and the margin of safety percentage for the original and flexed budget and the actual results. Make sure the Breakeven point is rounded appropriately.

(l) Format all values with the thousand separator and to zero decimal place. Font to Calibri 12, bold headings to the table, autofit cells.

SCENARIO 9

VLOOKUPS

Thelma Goody is the sales invoicing clerk for a VAT registered clothing wholesaler. Thelma prepares the sales invoices to be sent to the customer from the price list and a copy of the delivery note sent up to her by the sales department.

Today she has received the following delivery note from the sales department.

Delivery note: 2685

A B Fashions Ltd

To: Kids Clothes Ltd
9 Port Street
MANCHESTER
M1 5EX

3 Park Road
Parkway
Bristol
BR6 6SJ
Tel: 01272 695221
Fax: 01272 695222

Delivery date: 20 August 20X6

Quantity	Code	DESCRIPTION	Colour
90	SSB 330	Shawls (babies)	Assorted
30	CJA 991	Cashmere jumpers (adult)	Cream
30	GGC 442	Gloves (children)	Assorted

Received by:

Signature: Date:

(a) Download the **Creating an invoice** and using the price list and blank invoice create an invoice template for Thelma.

(b) You should insert Vlookups to pull information from the price list to the invoice and use an If statements to calculate the VAT where applicable.

SCENARIO 10

OVERHEADS

Ray Ltd has the following four production departments:

- Machining 1
- Machining 2
- Assembly
- Packaging

(a)   Download the **Overhead 1** file where you will find the budgeted overheads for Ray Ltd.

(b)   Create an overhead analysis sheet on the 'analysis' worksheet.

(c)   Using excel calculate the overhead for each department for depreciation and rent and rates (think about how absolute, relative and mixed referencing could be applied).

(d)   Use the copy and paste function to insert the indirect labour costs (think about a quick way to paste rather than having to do each value in turn).

(e)   Create a vlookup to assign the assembly costs to the assembly department.

(f)   Using formula/functions complete the overhead analysis sheet (round to the nearest £).

(g)   Format the cells to Arial size 12. Bold headings and thousand separator and zero decimal places.

SCENARIO 11

OVERHEADS 2

R Noble and Sons are a firm of agricultural engineers based in North Yorkshire.

They have a large workshop from which they operate. The business is divided into cost centres which include:

- Machining
- Fabrication
- Canteen
- Stores

(a)   Download the **Overhead 2** file where you will find the budgeted overheads for R Noble and Sons.

(b)   Open the analysis worksheet and create an overhead analysis table.

(c)   Using excel calculate the overhead for each department (think about how absolute, relative and mixed referencing could be applied).

(d)   Use an 'IF' function to re-apportion the overheads.

(e)   Use a function to round to the nearest £ where necessary.

(f)   Format to currency £ to zero decimal places.

SCENARIO 12

NPV

Whitby Engineering Factors are considering an investment in a new machine tool with an estimated useful life of five years.

The investment will require capital expenditure of £50,000.

(a)   Download the **NPV** file.

(b)   Using the data available calculate the NPV of the investment on the NPV worksheet:

(i)   Use copy and paste special to transpose the values into the NPV calculation from the data worksheet.

(ii)   Use formula for the calculation of net cash flow, discounted cash flow and net present value.

(iii)   Format monetary values as Number, zero decimal places and comma separator.

(c)   Use an 'IF' statement in cell B11 to state if based on the NPV the investment should go ahead. Format the font to red and bold.

(d)   Using the data in your NPV calculation calculate the payback period of the investment:

(i)   Use copy and paste special to input the values into the payback calculation.

(ii)   Use conditional formatting to highlight when the investment pays back.

(iii)   Format monetary values as Number, zero decimal places and comma separator.

(iv)   In cell K11 enter the number of years needed to payback.

(v)   In cell M11 use a formula to calculate the number of months ensuring you round appropriately.

SCENARIO 13

FINAL ACCOUNTS

(a)   Download the **Final accounts** file.

(b)   Complete the trial balance. Check that it balances.

(c)   Copy and paste the trial balance account names on to sheet 2. Use this to create a dropdown list for all the blue cells on the 'accounts' worksheet. To ensure that the appropriate terminology is used in the financial accounts you may need to change terms in the trial balance list on sheet 2. For example Sales ledger control account needs to be Trade receivables.

(d)   Rename sheet 2 'List'.

(e)   Complete the Statement of profit or loss on the accounts worksheet:

(i)   Insert formulas in cells G8, H9, H16 and H17 to allow totals to be calculated automatically as the statement is populated.

(ii)   Use a vlookup to enter the correct figures into the remaining blank cells from the trial balance. The use of absolute, relative and mixed referencing in the vlookup formula should enable you to cut and paste rather than hard entering the formula in each cell.

(f)   Complete the Statement of financial position on the accounts worksheet:

   (i)   Insert formulas in cells Q5, Q6, O7, P7, Q7, P14, O18, Q19, Q20 and Q25 to allow totals to be calculated automatically as the statement is populated.

   (ii)   Use a formula to enter the correct figure into cells P5, P6, P10, P11, O16 and Q24.

   (iii)   Use a vlookup to enter the correct figures into the remaining blank cells from the trial balance. The use of absolute, relative and mixed referencing in the vlookup formula should enable you to cut and paste rather than hard entering the formula in each cell.

(g)   Format the numbers to zero decimal places with a comma separator.

SCENARIO 14

PARTNERSHIP

Nick and Ted are in partnership sharing profits in the ratio of 3:2. During the year ended 30 June 20X4 the partnership made a profit of £120,000.

The partnership agreement states that Ted is to receive a salary of £20,000 and that interest on capital balances is paid at 6% per annum.

The balances on the current accounts, capital accounts and drawings accounts at the year-end before the appropriation of profit were as follows:

		£
Capital	Nick	150,000
	Ted	100,000
Current	Nick	3,000 (credit)
	Ted	1,000 (debit)
Drawings	Nick	56,000
	Ted	59,000

(a)   Download the **Partnership** file and complete the appropriation account and the partners' current accounts after appropriation of profit and transfer of drawings at 30 June 20X4. Use formulae where appropriate rather than hard entering the values.

Ted now asks what figure the profit for the year would need to be if he were to have a total amount distributed to him of £40,000. Assume all other data is unchanged.

(b)   Open a new worksheet and name it 'Goal Seek'.

(c)   In the partnership appropriation statement, use What if Goal Seek analysis to amend your data.

(d)   When the Goal Seek dialogue is showing and before you click OK take a screenshot. Complete the Goal Seek.

(e)   Go to the Goal Seek worksheet and paste the screen shot.

Section 3

ANSWERS TO EXAM – PART I PRACTICE TASKS

ETHICS

TASK 1.1

Assessment objective 1	Demonstrate an understanding of the relevance of the ethical code for accountants, the need to act ethically in a given situation, and the appropriate action to take in reporting questionable behaviour

TASK 1.2

Assessment objective 2	Prepare accounting records and respond to errors, omissions and other concerns, in accordance with accounting and ethical principles and relevant regulations

TASK 1.3

Assessment objective 4	Apply ethical and accounting principles when preparing final accounts for different types of organisation, develop ethical courses of action and communicate relevant information effectively

1 FIVE SCENARIOS

Scenario 1

The principle of confidentiality imposes an obligation on Alessandro to refrain from

using the information to the advantage of Sueka LLP'	✓
disclosing the information within Sueka LLP'	
disclosing the information to anyone at Polina Ltd'	

Scenario 2

Because she shows business acumen, offer her the job	
Because she has breached the fundamental principles of integrity and confidentiality, report her to the AAT	✓
Because she lacks integrity, inform her that she will not be offered the job	✓

Scenario 3

Objectivity and confidentiality	✓
Integrity and professional behaviour	
Confidentiality and professional competence	

Objectivity as Vernon has a conflict of interest – which is he representing?

Confidentiality as it would be very hard for Vernon not use the knowledge he has for one company when arguing for the other's position.

Scenario 4

Nothing	
Seek legal advice	
Advise Sam of relevant threats and safeguards that will protect Nick should he receive such an offer from Sam's organisation	✓
Immediately inform higher levels of management	

Scenario 5

	Yes	No
Continue with forging a relationship with the client		✓
Inform the client that without knowing the correct address the client/accountant relationship cannot be forged	✓	
Consider reporting the conversation to NCA	✓	

To comply with customer due diligence (part of money laundering regulations), the best course of action for Connor to take would be to inform the client that without knowing the correct address the client/accountant relationship cannot be forged.

The reluctance to disclose an address raises concerns over possible money laundering, so Connor must consider reporting the conversation to NCA.

2   JESS

Integrity	
Confidentiality	
Professional competence and due care	✓
Professional behaviour	
Objectivity	

3   NIGHT OUT

(a)

Integrity	
Confidentiality	
Professional competence and due care	
Professional behaviour	✓
Objectivity	

(b)

Do nothing – a sign is not worth losing your job over	
Suggest to the FD that he should replace the sign	✓

Bella should suggest to the Finance Director that he should replace the sign, and possibly discuss the matter with the Managing Director.

4   DILEMMA

(a)

Integrity	
Confidentiality	✓
Professional competence and due care	
Professional behaviour	
Objectivity	

(b)

From an ethical point of view you should tell your friend about the redundancies on the grounds it could save her unnecessary financial problems and distress.	
You should not tell your friend about the redundancies.	✓

You should not tell your friend about the redundancies as to do so would breach confidentiality.

5   JUSTIN

(a)

Self-interest threat	✓
Self-review threat	
Intimidation threat	
Advocacy threat	
Familiarity threat	

(b)

Continue as senior but make the partners aware of the inheritance	
Ask to be removed from the assignment	✓
Resign from Tipling LLP	
Report the matter to the National Crime Agency (NCA)	

6 PROCEDURE

(a)

| She should cooperate with the investigation | ✓ |
| She should refuse to cooperate as it would breach confidentiality | |

(b)

Misconduct	✓
Money laundering	
Whistleblowing	

(c)

Lose her job with C plc	
Be expelled from the Association	✓
Have her membership of the Association suspended	✓
Have her practicing licence withdrawn.	✓
Receive a prison sentence	
Have to re-sit all her professional exams	

7 MLRO

(a)

Breach of confidentiality	
Tipping off	✓
Money laundering	

(b) The maximum sentence is 5 years.

(c)

HMRC	
The National Crime Agency (NCA)	✓
The national press	

(d) £0 – De minimus means no minimum limit.

8   DONNA

	True	False
Funds retained after discovery of a tax error amount to money laundering by Stoppard plc	✓	
Donna should report the matter to the National Crime Agency (NCA)	✓	
Donna needs to make an authorised disclosure to the National Crime Agency NCA	✓	

Funds dishonestly retained after discovery of a tax error become criminal property so their retention amounts to money laundering by Stoppard plc.

As she is now aware of the error, Donna should report to the National Crime Agency (NCA) that she suspects Stoppard plc of money laundering because it has refused to notify the matter to HMRC. She will be protected from a claim for breach of confidentiality when making this report.

Knowing she may have been involved in money laundering, Donna needs to make an authorised disclosure to NCA which may help protect her from a charge that she herself, in making the error, was engaged in money laundering.

9   CODE OF ETHICS

	True	False
An accountant is under no duty to disclose the limitations of their expertise to the client		✓ (130.6)
An accountant is only responsible for his or her own professional qualifications and training		✓ (130.5)
An accountant may need to compromise the most precise attention to detail in preparing work in order to meet a reasonable deadline	✓ (130.4)	

130.6 of the Code of Ethics states that 'where appropriate, a professional accountant should make clients, employers or other users of the professional services aware of limitations inherent in the services to avoid the misinterpretation of an expression of opinion as an assertion of fact'.

130.5 of the Code of Ethics states that 'a professional accountant should take steps to ensure that those working under the professional accountant's authority in a professional capacity have appropriate training and supervision'.

130.4 of the Code of Ethics state that 'diligence encompasses the responsibility to act in accordance with the requirements of an assignment, carefully, thoroughly and on a timely basis'. Inevitably, diligence represents a balance between punctiliousness and punctuality!

10   INTEGRITY

All of these are potentially breaches of the principle of integrity. Even if information is freely available, it may not be clear that it is important in the context of the work undertaken. As such, the accountant may be misleading the client by leaving it to the client to find out something. Similarly, partial information may be highly misleading. Forgetting to mention important information, unless inadvertent, could be classed as being reckless. There is a duty to be careful that is bound up with the concept of integrity. Regardless of the duty of trust and confidence, the client should not be kept in the dark to avoid embarrassment. It may be in the latter circumstances, that some urgent consultations within the firm or with a regulator or legal advisers may be appropriate.

11 CONFIDENTIAL

B is correct. Although a client might request the disclosure of information, there may be certain circumstances when that information might include other confidential information, relating to another party. However, when refusing to disclose, reasons should be given and a second opinion in principle might be sought from the person responsible for Information and Data compliance in your organisations. Requests from the regulator, unless they are acting unlawfully, will normally be appropriate to disclose information.

Requests made by solicitors, are not in themselves, requests where there is a legal obligation to disclose. The reason for the request should be a reason where there is a legal or professional obligation to disclose or where the person requesting the information through the solicitor is the sole subject of it. Solicitors' letters should be dealt with in a courteous and timely way, but should not be assumed to have any greater weight in themselves than a request by any other member of the public.

Requests by your employer, other than as part of regulatory review or because the matter is being dealt with by a variety of people across the office, all subject to the same confidentiality, should be treated with care and should fall in the category of acceptable disclosures within the terms of your Data and Information Management procedures. Most damaging breaches of confidentiality occur as a result of internal disclosure where the recipient is unaware of the confidential nature of the material they are receiving.

12 THREATS

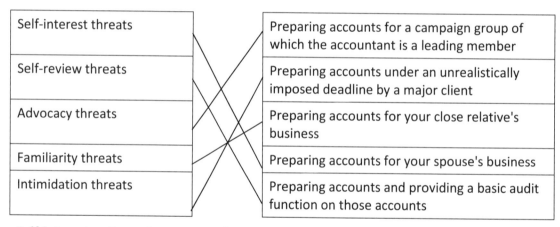

Self-interest – Preparing accounts for your spouse's business will clearly cause a personal conflict of interests.

Self-review – In this situation the accountant would be reviewing, as auditor, the work that they had themselves completed which would hinder their independence.

Advocacy – Being a member of the campaign group, the accountant will be seen to be advocating the group.

Familiarity – Preparing accounts for someone that you are very familiar with can put pressure on the accountant to act favourably towards, in this situation, their relative.

Intimidation – Not wanting to lose their major client, the accountant may feel intimidated into meeting the deadline at the cost of the accuracy of their work.

13   E

D is the correct answer

E stands to make a gain if he manipulates the figures to get a better bonus, hence E is in a position of a self-interest threat.

14   R

C is the correct answer

15   CX

(a)   A and D

According to the Code of ethics CX is in a position where she may be compromising her integrity and objectivity.

Integrity – This principle imposes an obligation to be truthful and honest on the accountant. A professional accountant should not be associated with reports or other information where she/he believes that the information contains misleading statements. This seems to be the case with the revised forecasts; CX believes that the revised forecasts are 'grossly overstated'.

Objectivity – A professional accountant should not allow conflict of interest or undue influence of others to override professional or business judgements or to compromise their professional judgements. The management board are overriding CX's professional and business judgement as they are imposing their assumptions on the forecast profits.

(b)

	Dealing with an ethical dilemma
1	Gather evidence and document the problem
2	Report internally to immediate management
3	Report internally to higher management
4	Report externally
5	Remove herself from the situation

16   RS

(a)   A and D

RS must also comply with the CIMA codes fundamental principles of integrity and objectivity. Changing the management information would breach both of these principles.

(b)   D

17 PRINCIPLES

Principle	*Interpretation*
Professional competence and due care	Maintaining a relevant level of professional knowledge and skills so that a competent service can be provided.
Professional behaviour	Complying with relevant laws and regulations.
Integrity	Being straightforward, honest and truthful in all professional and business relationships.
Confidentiality	Not disclosing information unless there is specific permission or a legal or professional duty to do so.
Objectivity	Not allowing bias, conflict of interest or the influence of other people to override professional judgement.

18 ACTION

C is the correct answer

The basic principle here is that of confidentiality. To go outside of the business and professional environment in this manner without first considering the other options presented would not be following recommended process.

A – AAT's ethics helpline exists to give members advice and is not a breach of confidentiality as it is within the professional arena. B – Reporting the company to the environment agency would comply with relevant legislation, however you would need to sure of your facts before whistle blowing. D – The Audit committee should be all NEDs and therefore a logical place to go, particularly as they are also responsible for the whistle blowing policy.

19 FUNDAMENTAL PRINCIPLES

Confidentiality	✓
Honesty	
Objectivity	✓
Respect	
Integrity	✓

20 ETHICS AND LAW

If a person complies with the letter of the law she will always be acting ethically.	
Ethics in business is the application of ethical values to business.	✓
If a company has a code of ethics this will eliminate the need for legislation.	

The law must always be obeyed but just obeying the law does not necessarily mean those actions are ethical. As a consequence of unethical behaviour the public could lose trust in the accounting profession but simply having a code of ethics will not eliminate the need for legislation; the code must be followed.

21   ISSUES

A is the correct answer

B, C and D options are examples of good governance rather than an ethical issue.

22   BREACHES

You have been told that one of your colleagues in the accounts department has regularly submitted inflated expenses claims. This is a breach of the fundamental principle of integrity.	
You are aware that a colleague in the accounts department regularly takes home reports to check and does so after a few cocktails. This is a breach of the fundamental principle of professional behaviour.	
You are employed as Management Accountant and have been asked to dismiss one of your colleagues for misconduct. You are aware that this is untrue and that the Company is trying to reduce the workforce without making the due redundancy payments. This is a breach of the fundamental principle of integrity.	✓

Option (1) is a breach of the fundamental principle of professional behaviour and option (2) is a breach of professional competence and due care.

23   AVOIDANCE

Both tax evasion and tax avoidance are illegal, but tax evasion involves providing HM Revenue and Customs with deliberately false information	
Tax evasion is illegal, whereas tax avoidance involves the minimisation of tax liabilities by the use of any lawful means	✓
Both tax evasion and tax avoidance are illegal, but tax avoidance involves providing HM Revenue and Customs with deliberately false information	
Tax avoidance is illegal, whereas tax evasion involves the minimisation of tax liabilities by the use of any lawful means	

Tutorial note

The term tax evasion summarises any action taken to avoid or reduce tax by illegal means, for example providing HM Revenue and Customs with deliberately false information.

24 DUMPING

Members have a duty of confidentiality.

However, there are occasions where the accountant has a professional or legal duty to disclose the information and therefore the breach of confidentiality is permissible.

Environmental damage is one such instance.

25 BENEFITS

(a)   The ethical principles potentially affected are as follows:

Integrity – How will Jacqui manage her personal interest with the need to be true and fair?

Objectivity – How will Jacqui manage her personal interest in the benefits package with the need to remain unbiased and consider only the relevant facts?

Professional Competence and Due Care – Does Jacqui have all the necessary skills to draw up such a package?

Professional Behaviour – How should Jacqui proceed so as not to bring discredit herself and the accountancy profession?

It would be very easy for Jacqui's recommendations to appear biased, even if she has acted ethically.

(b)   Jacqui should start by considering the following issues:

Identify relevant facts:

She should consider the organisation's policies, procedures and guidelines, accounting standards, best practices, code of ethics, applicable laws and regulations.

Is the information used for assessing the potential new benefits package independent? Who else has been involved in the proposal for the new benefits package?

Identify affected parties:

Key affected parties are Jacqui and the rest of the SMT. Other possible affected parties are employees, human resources, shareholders and financial backers.

Identify who should be involved in the resolution:

Jacqui should consider not just who should be involved, but also for what reason and timing of their involvement.

She could think about contacting the AAT for advice and guidance, or discuss the matter with trusted colleagues or someone from human resources.

(c)   **Possible courses of action**

Before explaining her findings to the SMT, it may be advisable for Jacqui to tell the SMT how she approached the project and who else was involved, for example, human resources.

She should declare her conflict of interest and not vote on the proposal for the new benefits package.

It may be advisable to involve human resources or another independent party to present the findings to the SMT. During the presentation, she should demonstrate how her findings were arrived at and who else was involved in the project.

26   SUSHIL

(a)   This situation presents an intimidation threat.

(b)   The best course of action would be to speak to his employer and explain that it is illegal to falsify the accounts.

27   TRUE

(a)   No, Naills as an AAT member has a duty to produce a true and fair view of the accounts.

(b)   The definition of false accounting is concealing or falsifying accounting records with a view to personal gain or providing false information that is misleading or deceptive.

28   MEERA

Matter 1

(a)   Fees

While some discounting of fees is seen as commercially acceptable way to win business, heavily discounted fees are perceived as a 'self-interest' threat to professional behaviour. This does not mean that they should be avoided at all costs but guidelines need to be followed.

Fees should reflect the value of the professional services performed for the client and there is a risk with low fees of a perception that the quality of work could be impaired.

Tax bill

Meera should consider the fundamental principle of Integrity.

It would be dishonest to promise to reduce a tax bill simply to gain a client when she believes the bill to be reasonable.

Matter 2

(b)   Meera should continue to advise Greg to contact the HMRC but it would be a breach of confidentiality for her to do so without his express permission, which seems unlikely in this case.

(c)   If Greg, after having had a reasonable time to reflect, does not correct the error, Meera should do the following:

•   Inform Greg that she/her firm can no longer act for him because funds dishonestly retained after discovery of a tax error become criminal property so their retention amounts to money laundering by Greg.

•   Make an internal report on the matter to her firm's MLRO.

29   RS

(a)   The fundamental principles of integrity and objectivity are being threated here. Changing the management information would breach both of these principles.

(b)   The offers of incentives make this a self-interest threat as RS stands to benefit if he/she changes the figures.

30 DISMISS

The Public Interest Disclosure Act 1998 (PIDA) protects individuals from dismissal who disclose confidential information, whether internally or to a prescribed regulator when given in good faith.

Sarah is thus protected under the PIDA.

31 MLC

MLC have clearly positioned themselves as an ethical company and will therefore attract shareholders who are looking for ethical investments and customers looking for ethically produced goods.

If they continue trading with this supplier then their reputation will suffer if the news gets out.

By taking strong decisive action and controlling the news story they have demonstrated that they follow their stated ethical principles.

The best response would thus be to "Cancel all contracts with the supplier and release a press statement stating how the company will always act quickly and decisively if unethical practices are suspected."

32 STEPHANIE

Integrity

Integrity implies that a person should be straightforward and honest in all business relationships. The management accountant is not being honest because he is helping to produce budgets he knows to be inaccurate.

Objectivity

By taking the football tickets in exchange for altering figures the management accountant is allowing bias to override business judgements.

Professional competence and due care

The management accountant's skills are not under question and so this principle does not appear to have been breached.

Confidentiality

The management accountant does not appear to have breached confidentiality. The conversations Stephanie overheard involved Alpha staff and so no information has been leaked.

Professional behaviour

The management accountant has not behaved professionally and in line with AAT expectations. In addition to using incorrect figures in the budgets he has tried to influence Stephanie to do the same.

33 REFERENCE

(a) The ethical principles involved here are as follows:

- **Integrity** – Steve must be straightforward and honest in all professional and business relationships. Integrity also implies fair dealing and truthfulness and there is a danger that the reference is not a fair or true representation of the facts as he sees them.

- **Objectivity** – the large fee should not be allowed to colour Steve's judgement. This presents a self-interest threat.

  It could also be argued that, because Kept Ltd is Steve's oldest client, then there is also a familiarity threat to objectivity.

- **Professional behaviour** – writing a reference that Steve suspects to be false could bring discredit to himself and the profession.

(b) Steve is potentially guilty of 'fraud by false representation' under the Fraud Act 2006. This is where a person makes 'any representation as to fact or law ... express or implied' which they know to be untrue or misleading.

There is also the possibility that the large fee could be interpreted as a bribe under the Bribery Act 2010 and Steve could be found guilty of passive bribery (receiving a bribe) under the Act.

(c) It is acceptable practice for Steve to include a disclaimer of liability and it certainly does no harm to include one. However, disclaimers can be challenged in court so may not afford Steve any protection.

If he has serious doubts over whether or not Kept Ltd will be able to pay the rent, then he shouldn't write the reference.

34 KUTCHINS

Gemma is allowed to use general knowledge and experience from a previous employer but NOT specific information from that employer that is covered by the duty of confidentiality.

This means that general accountancy, audit and management skills and knowledge can all be used but not specific information concerning Kirk Ltd.

35 BEVIS

Matter 1

Bevis should NOT tell the Managing Director anything that would be considered 'private information' as this would be a breach of confidentiality.

Matter 2

Bevis should tell the customer that he has been unable to gain the information.

Pretending to be a customer lacks integrity and would not be acting professionally.

36 JULIE

(a) This situation presents a self-interest threat.

(b) Two safeguards the assurance firm should have in place are:

- A policy requiring the immediate disclosure of such an offer of employment
- A policy requiring Julie to be removed from the assurance engagement.

37 NO DEFENCE

(a) The Bribery Act 2010 creates four offences:

1 bribing a person to induce or reward them to perform a relevant function improperly

2 requesting, accepting or receiving a bribe as a reward for performing a relevant function improperly

3 using a bribe to influence a foreign official to gain a business advantage

4 a new form of corporate liability for failing to prevent bribery on behalf of a commercial organisation.

(b) For a commercial organisation, it is a defence to have in place 'adequate procedures' to prevent bribery.

This may include implementing anti-bribery procedures.

It is important that firms consider what procedures are 'adequate' for their firm given the risks they face and the way they run their business. The procedures should be proportionate to the risk posed.

For some firms there will be no need to put bribery prevention procedures in place as there is no risk of bribery on their behalf. Other firms may need to put measures in place in key areas, such as gifts and hospitality, as this is the area where they have identified a risk.

Corporate ignorance of individual wrongdoing will provide no protection against prosecution.

(c) Certainly the excessive nature of the hospitality would mean that it would be viewed as an attempt to bribe the MP concerned.

While M plc could argue that they are not guilty of 1, 2 and 3 above, they are likely to be found guilty under offence 4.

Even though Mr Igbinadola was an agent and not an employee and even though the Board claim ignorance, the company could still be found guilty of failing to prevent bribery.

The only possible defence would be to demonstrate that they had adequate procedures in place to prevent bribery, but in this case it looks difficult to prove this.

38 L PLC

Arguing that an activity complies with 'local law' or 'customs and practices' is no defence under the Bribery Act.

If L plc goes ahead with the request, then two offences under the Act will have been committed:

1 Using a bribe (the donations) to influence a foreign official to gain a business advantage.

2 Failing to prevent bribery on behalf of a commercial organisation.

L plc should thus refuse the request for 'donations'.

39 IN-HOUSE CODE

The code is a voluntary one prepared by John Grooms Ltd for its own use.

It cannot insist on suppliers adopting it.

The code cannot be statutory since that would be created under legislation/regulation/case law and used by many companies.

40 NEW CODE

1   *All products should be purchased from local farms and suppliers where appropriate.*

This would have a positive impact from a sustainability perspective as it would reduce distribution miles and the associated impact on fossil fuels and pollution.

The main reservation is the wording 'where appropriate' as there is no indication as to what 'appropriate' means – for example, Cosby could buy cheaper goods from overseas suppliers and argue that the low cost made it 'appropriate'.

2   *All packing materials should be obtained from renewable sources where feasible.*

This would also have a positive impact from a sustainability perspective as it would reduce deforestation to provide cardboard and paper packaging.

The main reservation is the wording 'where feasible' as there is no indication as to what 'feasible' means – for example, Cosby could buy cheaper goods with plastic packaging and argue that the low cost made it 'feasible'.

3   *All suppliers to be paid on time.*

This should mean that suppliers are treated fairly. However, there is no indication that suppliers have any say in what constitutes 'on time'.

4   *All suppliers to be paid fair prices as determined by the Purchasing Manager.*

This should also mean that suppliers are treated fairly.

However, there is no indication that suppliers have any say in what constitutes 'fair prices' – the price needs to be seen to be reasonable and fair by both parties.

41 CHRIS

(a)   This situation represents a threat to the fundamental principles of

- Objectivity – because it is difficult to act without a perception of bias when the two clients' interests are in such conflict because they both want a price and terms beneficial to themselves; and

- Confidentiality – because he has confidential information in respect of each client.

(b)   Chris should:

- consider relevant facts/ethical issues involved/his fundamental principles/any established procedures in HJK and Co

- establish alternative courses of action, establish which is most consistent with the fundamental principles and establish the consequences of each

- seek advice about the matter within HJK and Co, and document the substance of the issue and discussions.

(c)   In acting for one of the clients Chris should consider instituting appropriate safeguards so that his familiarity with the other client does not affect his professional judgement/objectivity, and so that he does not breach confidentiality re the other party.

42 SIMON

(a) This situation represents a self-interest threat.

(b) Simon's best course of action is to sell the shares or, failing that, to ask to be removed from the audit engagement.

43 LAST

(a) This situation displays a breach of Confidentiality.

(b) Jason's friend, Brian, should talk to the director concerned and explained that to act in the way suggested would be unethical.

   (**Note:** you could have answered that he should get advice without breaching confidentiality, say by ringing the AAT ethics helpline.)

(c) Brian should resign and state the reason for the resignation. Then report the situation to the external regulators.

44 SAFE AND SOUND

Matter A

The ethical threat is basically one of self-interest.

The director is using price sensitive information to ensure that a loss is prevented by selling shares now rather than after the announcement of poor results for the company.

One ethical safeguard would be a professional code of conduct that requires directors to carry out their duties with integrity and therefore in the best interests of the shareholders. The director would recognise that selling the shares would start the share price falling already and this would not benefit the shareholders.

As a code it may not be effective – the director could argue that selling shares prior to the results was designed to warn shareholders of the imminent fall in share price and was, therefore, in their best interests.

An alternative course of action is to ban trading in shares a given number of weeks prior to the announcement of company results (as happens in the USA where directors are not allowed to sell shares during 'blackout periods'). This would be effective as share sales can be identified and the directors could incur a penalty for breach of legislation.

Matter B

The ethical threat appears to be a lack of independence and self-interest regarding the setting of remuneration for these directors.

Not only do they have common directorships, but they are also good friends. They could easily vote for higher than normal remuneration packages for each other on the remuneration committees knowing that the other director will reciprocate on the other remuneration committee.

In corporate governance terms, one ethical safeguard is to ban these cross-directorships.

The ban would be enforceable as the directors of companies must be stated in annual accounts, hence it would be easy to identify cross-directorships. The ban would also be effective as the conflict of interest would be removed.

In professional terms, the directors clearly have a conflict of interest. While their professional code of ethics may mention this precisely as an ethical threat, Graham and Mike should follow the spirit of the code and resign their non-executive directorships.

This again would remove the threat.

Matter C

There is a clear ethical threat to the directors of Company Z.

They appear to be being bribed so that they do not query the management style of the chairman. The threat is that the directors will simply accept the benefits given to them rather than try to run Company Z in the interests of the shareholders. It is clearly easy to accept that option.

Ethical safeguards are difficult to identify and their application depends primarily on the desire of the directors to take ethical actions. In overall terms, the chairman does not appear to be directly breaching ethical or governance codes. The main safeguard is therefore for the directors not to accept appointment as director to Company Z or resign from the board if already a director.

The director could attempt to get the matter discussed at board level, although it is unlikely the chairman would allow this. Taking any other action is in effect 'whistle blowing' on all the directors and has the negative impact that the director would also have to admit to receiving 'benefits' from the company.

45 FREE HOLIDAYS

The Bribery Act 2010 creates four offences:

1   bribing a person to induce or reward them to perform a relevant function improperly

2   requesting, accepting or receiving a bribe as a reward for performing a relevant function improperly

3   using a bribe to influence a foreign official to gain a business advantage

4   a new form of corporate liability for failing to prevent bribery on behalf of a commercial organisation.

Leigh Davis is guilty of bribery (offence 1 above) under the Act as he is bribing Sarah by offering her free holidays in return for her performing her function as an audit manager improperly.

Sarah is guilty of receiving a bribe (offence 2 above) from Leigh Davis.

B & Sons LLP could also be guilty of bribery of the Act for failing to prevent bribery (offence 4 above) unless they can show that they had in place 'adequate procedures'.

Both Leigh and Sarah could receive a maximum jail sentence of up to ten years.

If B & Sons LLP is found guilty they could be liable for an unlimited fine.

46 KEN

(a) Money laundering is the process by which the proceeds of crime, either money or other property, are converted into assets, which appear to have a legitimate rather than an illegal origin. The aim of the process is to disguise the source of the property, in order to allow the holder to enjoy it free from suspicion as to its source.

The Proceeds of Crime Act 2002 (POCA) seeks to control money laundering by creating three categories of criminal offences in relation to the activity.

Laundering

Under the POCA, the three money laundering offences are

- s327 – Concealing, disguising, converting, transferring or removing criminal property.

- s328 – Taking part in an arrangement to facilitate the acquisition, use or control of criminal property.

- s329 – Acquiring, using or possessing criminal property.

These offences are punishable on conviction by a maximum of 14 years' imprisonment and/or a fine.

Failure to report

The second category of offence relates to failing to report a knowledge or suspicion of money laundering.

It is an offence for a person who knows or suspects that another person is engaged in money laundering not to report the fact to the appropriate authority.

However, the offence only relates to individuals, such as accountants, who are acting in the course of business in the regulated sector.

The offences set out in these sections are punishable on conviction by a maximum of five years' imprisonment and/or a fine.

Tipping off

The third category of offence relates to tipping off. It is an offence to make a disclosure which is likely to prejudice any investigation under the Act.

The offences set out in these sections are punishable on conviction by a maximum of five years' imprisonment and/or a fine.

(b) Ken would therefore be guilty of the primary offence of money laundering as explained in the section above.

Los is also guilty of an offence in relation to the Proceeds of Crime Act as he is clearly assisting Ken in his money laundering procedure. He is actively concealing and disguising criminal property, and his arrangement with Ken facilitates the retention of criminal property.

Mel is equally guilty under the same provisions as Los, in that he is actively engaged in the money laundering process, by producing false accounts.

AVBK, FAPR, ETHICS

TASK 1.2

Assessment objective 2	Prepare accounting records and respond to errors, omissions and other concerns, in accordance with accounting and ethical principles and relevant regulations

TASK 1.3

Assessment objective 4	Apply ethical and accounting principles when preparing final accounts for different types of organisation, develop ethical courses of action and communicate relevant information effectively

TASK 1.5

Assessment objective 5	Prepare financial accounting information, comprising extended trial balances

47   BESS

Sales ledger control account

20X7		£	20X7		£
01 Sep	Balance b/d	188,360	01 Sep	Balance b/d	2,140
30 Sep	Sales		30 Sep	Sales returns	9,160
	(101,260 + 1,360) (ii)	102,620		Cash received	91,270
	Cash refunds	300		Cash discounts	1,430
	Petty cash refund (iii)	20		Irrecoverable debts written off	460
	Balance c/d (W1)	3,320		Contras (480 + 500)	980
				Balance c/d	189,180
		294,620			294,620

Purchases ledger control account

20X7		£	20X7		£
01 Sep	Balance b/d	120	01 Sep	Balance b/d	89,410
30 Sep	Purchases returns	4,280	30 Sep	Purchases	
				(68,420 – 1,360) (ii)	67,060
	Cash to suppliers	71,840		Balance carried down	90
	Cash discounts	880			
	Contras (480 + 500)	980			
	Balance carried down	78,460			
		156,560			156,560

(W1) **Sales ledger credit balances**

	£
Draft closing balance	3,360
Wrong way adjustment of £20 refund	(40)
	3,320

48 SALLY

(a) **Journals**

		Dr £	Cr £
(i)	Sally Ltd purchase ledger control	1,080	
	Sally Ltd sales ledger control		1,080
	(Being contra settlement)		
(ii)	Irrecoverable debts expense	3,590	
	Sales ledger control		3,590
	(Being irrecoverable debts written off)		
(iii)	Allowance for doubtful debts adjustment (5,200 – 3,060)	2,140	
	Allowance for doubtful debts		2,140
	(Being an increase in the allowance for doubtful debts)		
(iv)	AUE Ltd sales ledger	200	
	AUT Ltd sales ledger		200
	(Being correction of misposted cash receipt)		

(b) **Receivables**

	£
Sales ledger balance	384,600
Contra settlement (i)	(1,080)
Irrecoverable debt write offs (ii)	(3,590)
	379,930
Less Allowance for doubtful debts (iii)	(5,200)
Receivables	374,730

49 GEORGE

(a) Annual depreciation charge   =   £8,400 × 15%

                                      =   £1,260

	£
Cost	8,400
Less: depreciation (1,260 × 19/12)	(1,995)
Carrying amount	**6,405**

The asset was owned for a total of 19 months between 1 May 20X0 and 1 December 20X1. As it was sold on the 1 December 20X1 i.e. at the beginning of the month, that month does not incur a depreciation charge. If the asset had been sold on the 31 December 20X1 there would be a month's depreciation for December 20X1.

(b) **Loss** on disposal   =   £6,405 – £6,000

                        =   **£405**

A loss on disposal was made as the sales proceeds were £405 less than the carrying amount.

50 NON-CURRENT ASSETS 1

Narrative	Dr	Cr
Disposals	12,000	
Vehicles at cost		12,000
Vehicles accumulated depreciation	9,119	
Disposals		9,119
Vehicles at cost	15,250	
Motor vehicle expenses	210	
Disposals		3,800
Sundry payables		11,660
Totals	36,579	36,579

51 NON-CURRENT ASSETS 2

(a) Year ended 31/12/X1 £20,000 × 10% = £2,000

Year ended 31/12/X2 (£20,000 – £2,000) × 10% = £1,800

Year ended 31/12/X3 (£20,000 – £2,000 – £1,800) × 10% = £1,620

Total accumulated depreciation (£2,000 + £1,800 + £1,620) = £5,420

(b)

Narrative	Dr	Cr
Disposals account	20,000	
Machinery cost account		20,000
Machinery accumulated depreciation account	5,420	
Disposals account		5,420
Bank	10,000	
VAT Control (20/120 × £10,000)		1,667
Disposals account (100/120 × £10,000)		8,333
Totals	35,420	35,420

Disposals

Machinery at cost	20,000	Machinery accumulated depreciation	5,420
		Bank	8,333
		Loss on disposal	6,247
	20,000		20,000

The profit or loss on disposal can also be calculated by comparing the sales proceeds to the carrying amount. The sales proceeds are £8,333 compared to a carrying amount of £14,580. Therefore, a loss of £6,247 has been made.

52 MATTRESS

Task 1

JOURNAL		Dr £	Cr £
(a)	Motor expenses	150	
	Motor vehicle at cost		150
(b)	Suspense	400	
	VAT (sales tax) account		400
(c)	Disposal account	11,000	
	Fixtures and fittings at cost		11,000
	Accumulated depreciation (F&F)	4,400	
	Disposal account		4,400
	Suspense	7,000	
	Disposal account		7,000
	Disposal account	400	
	Statement of profit or loss account (gain)		400
(d)	Suspense	3,600	
	Sales		3,600
(e)	Suspense	2,510	
	Bank		2,510

Task 2

Suspense account

	£		£
Journal (b)	400	Balance b/d	13,510
Journal (c)	7,000		
Journal (d)	3,600		
Journal (e)	2,510		
	———		———
	13,510		13,510

53 YEAR-END 1

(a)

	£	Debit	Credit
Accruals	4,820		4,820
Prepayments	2,945	2,945	
Motor expenses	572	572	
Administration expenses	481	481	
Light and heat	1,073	1,073	
Revenue	48,729		48,729
Purchases	26,209	26,209	
SLCA	5,407	5,407	
PLCA	3,090		3,090
Rent	45	45	
Purchase returns	306		306
Discounts allowed	567	567	
Capital	10,000		10,000
Loan	15,000		15,000
Interest paid	750	750	
Drawings	4,770	4,770	
Motor vehicles – cost	19,000	19,000	
Motor vehicle – acc. depreciation	2,043		2,043
VAT control	2,995		2,995
Wages	20,000	20,000	
Suspense account		**5,164**	
Totals		86,983	86,983

(b)

		Dr £	Cr £
(i)	Suspense	5,000	
	Capital		5,000
(ii)	Suspense	385	
	Sales ledger control account		385
(iii)	VAT	193	
	Suspense		193
(iv)	Rent	4,500	
	Suspense		4,500
	Rent	4,500	
	Suspense		4,500
(v)	Electricity	1,356	
	Suspense		1,356

54 ETB 1

Extended trial balance

Ledger account	Ledger balances		Adjustments	
	Dr £	Cr £	Dr £	Cr £
Accruals		1,330		300
Advertising	1,800			
Bank	7,912			
Capital		50,000		
Closing inventory			11,890	11,890
Depreciation charge				
Drawings	14,700			
Fixtures and fittings – accumulated depreciation		945		
Fixtures and fittings – cost	6,099			
Irrecoverable debts	345			
Allowance for doubtful debt adjustment				295
Electricity	1,587		300	
Loan	10,000			
Opening inventory	5,215			

				12,500	
Prepayment				12,500	
Allowance for doubtful debts		485	295		
Purchases	78,921				
Purchase returns					2,000
PLCA		14,000	2,400		
Rent	25,000				12,500
Revenue		145,825			
SLCA	9,500				
VAT control account		11,453			400
Wages	62,959				
	224,038	224,038	27,385		27,385

Key answer tips

(a) SLCA 9,500 × 2% = 190. Allowance currently 485, therefore debit with £295 to make it equal £190

(c) The prepayment for the year end is 10/12 × 15,000 = 12,500. For November and December X5 = 2/12 × 15,000 = 2,500. Total rental charge for the year = (10/12 × 12,000) + 2,500 = £12,500

(e) Accrual for November and December. 2/3 × 450 = £300

55 ETB 2

Extended trial balance

Ledger account	Ledger balances		Adjustments		Statement of profit or loss		Statement of financial position	
	Dr £	Cr £	Dr £	Cr £	Dr £	Cr £	Dr £	Cr £
Accruals		2,300		425				2,725
Advertising	1,800				1,800			
Bank	7,912		1,175				9,087	
Capital		40,000						40,000
Closing inventory			6,590	6,590		6,590	6,590	
Depreciation charge			821		821			
Drawings	14,700						14,700	
Fixtures and fittings – accumulated depreciation		945		821				1,766
Fixtures and fittings – cost	6,099						6,099	
Interest	345				345			
Light and heat	1,587		706		2,293			

Loan		10,000						10,000
Opening inventory	5,215				5,215			
Prepayments	485		927	281			1,131	
Purchases	75,921				75,921			
PLCA		14,000						14,000
Rent and rates	38,000			927	37,073			
Revenue		145,825				145,825		
SLCA	9,500			1,175			8,325	
VAT control account		11,453						11,453
Wages	62,959				62,959			
Loss						34,012	34,012	
	224,523	224,523	10,219	10,219	186,427	186,427	79,944	79,944

56   INCOMPLETE 1

(a)   £55,200

(b)   **Receivables (Sales ledger) control account**

Balance b/d	4,120	Bank	53,610
Credit sales	55,200	Balance c/d	5,710
	59,320		59,320

(c)   £254,400

(d)   **Bank account**

Balance b/d	5,630	Payroll expenses	48,000
SLCA	53,610	Administration expenses	6,400
Cash sales	254,400	Vehicle running costs	192,000
		Drawings	41,800
		Sales tax	17,300
		Balance c/d	8,140
	313,640		313,640

57   INCOMPLETE 2

£4,000

58 INCOMPLETE 3

(a) £1,280,000 × 75/100 = £960,000

(b) £960,000 − (£970,200 − £98,006) = £87,806

59 SOLE TRADER 1

Vincent Trading			
Statement of financial position as at 30 June 20X8			
	£	£	£
Non-current assets	**Cost**	**Depreciation**	**Carrying amount**
Equipment	17,500	4,500	13,000
Current assets			
Inventory		7,850	
Trade receivables (£7,800 − £840)		6,960	
Prepayments		3,200	
		18,010	
Current liabilities			
Payables (£6,800 + £1,450)	8,250		
VAT	2,950		
Accruals	750		
Bank	1,250		
		13,200	
Net current assets			4,810
Net assets			17,810
Financed by:			
Opening capital			17,000
Add: Net profit			8,810
Less: Drawings			8,000
Closing capital			17,810

60   SOLE TRADER 2

Beale – Statement of financial position as at 30 June 20X6			
	£	£	£
Non-current assets	Cost	Depreciation	Carrying amount
Motor vehicles	45,000	20,000	25,000
Current assets			
Inventory		17,500	
Trade receivables (£68,550 – £1,450)		67,100	
Cash		500	
		85,100	
Current liabilities			
Bank	2,250		
Trade payables	23,750		
Accruals	3,150		
VAT	3,500		
		32,650	
Net current assets			52,450
Net assets			77,450
Financed by:			
Opening capital			85,000
Less: Net loss			4,350
Less: Drawings			3,200
Closing capital			77,450

61   PARTNER 1

Partnership appropriation account for the year ended 30 June 20X9

	£
Profit for the year	220,000
Salaries:	
Gertrude	–18,000
Eddie	0
Polonius	–36,000
Interest on capital:	
Gertrude	–2,000
Eddie	–2,000
Polonius	–2,000
Sales commission:	
Gertrude	–8,250
Eddie	–6,800
Polonius	–4,715
Profit available for distribution	140,235
Profit share:	
Gertrude(40% × £140,235)	56,094
Ed (40% × £140,235)	56,094
Polonius (20% × £140,235)	28,047
Total residual profit distributed	140,235

62   PARTNER 2

(a)

Account name	Dr	Cr
Goodwill	£105,000	
Capital account – Cordelia		£36,750
Capital account – Goneril		£68,250

(b)   £31,750

New goodwill value   = £105,000 + £22,000

= £127,000

× 25%   = £31,750

63 PARTNER 3

Capital account – Will

Bank	31,000	Balance b/d	9,000
		Goodwill	15,000
		Current account	7,000
	31,000		31,000

64 INTEGRITY

Appropriate responses include the following:

Internal action

- Discuss the matter with the Finance Director to see if there is a valid case for posting this journal. From the information given, this seems unlikely.

External action

If the FD refuses to change the request and Frankie still feels uncomfortable, then he could:

- Go to the company's auditors to discuss the matter

- Seek guidance from the AAT.

Ultimately if the situation is not resolved, then he should consider resigning.

Note: The wrong answer here is to suggest that he should post the journal without question as the Finance director is his senior. This is NOT an appropriate action.

65 SUSTENANCE

(a)   The role of accountants

The roles of professional accountants in contributing to sustainability include the following:

- Challenging conventional assumptions of doing business.

- Redefining success.

- Establishing appropriate performance targets.

- Encouraging and rewarding the right behaviours.

- Ensuring that information flows that support decisions, and which monitor and report performance, go beyond the traditional ways of thinking about economic success.

Being sustainable requires the organisation to take full account of its impact on the planet and its people.

(b)   Impact on profit

An increased emphasis on sustainability can result in improved profits for the following reasons:

- Potential cost savings – e.g. due to lower energy usage.

- Short term gain in sales – e.g. if customers are influenced by sustainability-related labels on products.

- Long term gain in sales – e.g. due to enhanced PR and reputation.

- Better risk management – e.g. pre-empting changes in regulations may save compliance costs.

66 TIO RINO

Mining companies can try to be sustainable by adopting the following:

Social issues ('people')

- Provide a safe and healthy workplace for employees where their rights and dignity are respected.

- Build enduring relationships with local communities and neighbours that demonstrate mutual respect, active partnership, and long-term commitment.

- Improve safety record re accident, fatalities.

- Develop health programmes for local communities – e.g. in respect of AIDS/HIV in some African countries.

- Ensure that if communities need to be moved or relocated, that resettlement and compensation are generous and cultural heritage is not compromised.

- Invest in people over the long term by fostering diversity, providing challenging and exciting work and development opportunities, and rewarding for performance.

- Ensure post-mining land use is discussed with local communities and is consistent with their aims and needs.

Environmental issues ('planet')

- Wherever possible prevent – or otherwise minimise, mitigate and remediate – harmful effects of activities on the environment.

- Avoid developing sites where the risk to biodiversity is particularly high.

- Develop new ways to reduce emissions of dangerous gases such as SO_2 and NO_2.

- Plant new trees elsewhere to replace ones felled for mining to ensure biodiversity.

- Landscape and replant sites after mining has finished. Pay for species to be repopulated.

- Use offsetting schemes to compensate for emission of greenhouse gases (e.g. schemes to plant additional trees somewhere else).

- Develop ways to process waste to avoid polluting the surrounding water system.

- Reducing energy usage by more efficient processes.

- Recycle as much waste products as possible.

Economic issues ('Profit')

- Pay taxes without finding loopholes to avoid them.

- Ensure local communities benefit in terms of employments and a share of overall profits.

- Reinvest in local communities and projects rather than taking all profits back to the mining company's home country.

67 HOGGS FURNITURE

(a) Sustainable development is defined as 'development that meets the needs of the present without compromising the ability of future generations to meet their own needs' *(The UN's Bruntland Report).*

Sustainability is thus more than just looking at environmental concerns. It relates to the continuity of **economic**, **social** and **environmental** aspects of human society.

Another way of looking at this is that sustainable businesses offer products and services that fulfil society's needs while placing an equal emphasis on people, planet and profits.

(b) Areas that Jacob should appraise in order to answer the client's concerns include the following:

- Whether non-renewable hard woods are used in manufacture.

  The client would want reassurance that all materials are form renewable sources.

- The energy efficiency and level of emission of greenhouse gases due to the operation of the factory.

  While these cannot be eliminated altogether, the client would want to see evidence that Hoggs has taken steps to improve energy efficiency (e.g. thermal insulation, double glazing, installation of solar panels, etc) or uses carbon offset schemes.

- Treatment of staff

  Sustainability is not just about environmental issues but also incorporates social (people) aspects. The client may want to know what Hoggs' record is concerning accidents, staff development, diversity, etc.

- Tax

  Economic sustainability includes factors such as whether the company is paying tax and so contributing to the local/national community.

(c) Other ways Jacob can contribute to sustainability through his role as an accountant includes the following:

- Helping create an ethics-based culture in Hoggs.

- By championing and promoting sustainability.

- By highlighting the risks of not acting sustainably and draw attention to reputational and other ethical risks.

- By incorporating targets and performance measures consistent with a Triple Bottom Line (TBL) approach.

68   STEVEN

In respect of a genuine oversight, be it yours or a colleague's, AAT's code of ethics recognises that this can happen as long as the issue is promptly addressed and safeguards put in place.

It is possible to add an addendum about the incorrect note and this is the most expedient action.

However, it would be advisable first to consult with N&Q's auditors for their guidance on how best to proceed.

If the accounts do not "represent the facts accurately and completely in all material respects" you should not sign them, nor should the MD.

69   FINANCE

Option 1

Difference 1 – Limited liability – with a company a shareholder's liability is limited to any sums unpaid on shares issued, whereas with a partnership the partners are fully liable for business debts.
Difference 2 – Regulation/administration – companies must comply with the Companies Act and register with Companies House. Regulations for partnerships are less onerous.
Difference 3 – Taxation – companies pay tax in their own right whereas partnership profits are split between partners according to a profit sharing ratio and added to partners' individual taxable income.
Implication for finance 1 – The limited liability with a company may make it easier to attract potential shareholders than potential partners as they will perceive the investment to be less risky.
Implication for finance 2 – It's easier to spread ownership across a wide number of owners if issuing shares, rather than admitting new partners every time, again making attracting investors and raising finance easier.

Option 2

THREE elements of a SOFP that a bank would be interested in and why

Aspect of SOFP		Reason why the bank would look at this
1	Non-current assets	To assess whether the business has sufficient quality assets (e.g. land and buildings) to offer as security on a new loan. If it hasn't, then the bank may either refuse the loan or insist on higher interest rates to compensate for the extra risk.
2	Net current assets/ liabilities	To asses liquidity and, therefore, the business's ability to pay loan interest and repayments.
3	Loans	If a business already has a high level of loans (gearing), then the bank may feel it is too risky to lend it additional loans.

THREE stakeholders (other than a bank) who would use a SOFP and why

Stakeholder	Why they would use the SOFP
1 Potential suppliers	To assess the firm's ability to pay its creditors by looking at liquidity and, therefore, to decide whether or not to grant it credit.
2 Potential customers	To assess the financial stability of the business to evaluate its long term prospects before committing to any long term contracts.
3 Existing shareholders/ owners	To assess the value of their investment in the business – for example, to assess whether the business could afford them taking out drawings or paying out a dividend.
4 Potential investors	To assess the financial stability of the business to help decide whether or not to invest.

Note: only three required

70   ACCOUNTING FUNDAMENTALS

(1) The accounting equation

The accounting equation is as follows:

Assets – Liabilities = Capital + Profit – Drawings

Or rearranged:

Assets = Liabilities + Capital + Profit – Drawings

The equation is important as it is testing the basic principles of double entry- if the double entry has been done correctly (i.e. each transaction has at least 2 effects) then the equation will always balance.

If you look at the second equation above you can see that the equation is the same as the Balance sheet/Statement of Financial position. So the accounting equation is being used to check double entry and to also produce the SOFP.

(2) The statement of profit and loss

The statement of profit and loss (SPL) shows how well a business has performed over a period of time. It compares revenue earned (i.e. sales) with various expenses incurred to calculate the overall profit for a period. This is usually for a year but can be different.

The first section of the profit or loss is called the trading section as it shows the pure profit from the trade of the business (i.e. sales less costs of sales = gross profit). Beneath the gross profit all the expenses of the business are deducted to give the net profit for the year.

The SPL is produced using the accruals/matching basis, so for example we compare sales with costs of goods sold in order to calculate gross profit. Another example is where expenses incurred (for example telephone) are charged to the SPL even though we may not have paid for them. This is so that the SPL can accurately show all the revenues earned in a year and match them against the expenses incurred in a year (regardless of whether the cash has been paid/received).

The SPL is important as it informs the users of accounts as to whether the business has been successful in making profit for the period. It also (as mentioned above) shows whether the profit from the pure trade (gross profit) is sufficient to cover the expenses of the business.

It is used by different users or stakeholders of a business in making decisions. For examples investors may choose to invest in a business that it making healthy profits. Or a bank may decide to lend to a business that is making healthy profits as it is confident that it will receive the interest payments.

(3) The statement of financial position

The Statement of Financial position (SFP) provides a snapshot of a business's strength or financial position at one point in time. This is usually at the end of the year.

It lists the assets of the business – these are split between non-current assets (for examples land and buildings that the business expects to use over more than a year) and also current assets (for example inventory and cash). The SFP also lists amounts owed/liabilities and these are also split between noncurrent liabilities and current liabilities. The non-current liabilities are those due after more than 1 year (for example a 10 year bank loan) and the current liabilities are due within a year (i.e. trade payables). The SFP also shows the capital section which are amounts due back to the owner. As per the accounting equation the capital section will show capital + profit – drawings.

The SFP is important as it shows the assets/liabilities position at one point in time. (It also shows the amount owed back to the owner i.e. capital). It shows the financial strength of the business (i.e. do the assets exceed liabilities?). It also shows how the business has been financed (i.e. has the bank lent the business a large amount of money?) It also shows the liquidity position of the business (see below).

It is used by different stakeholders/users of the accounts to make decisions. For example a bank may look at the business SFP and see that it already has a large loan liability on the SFP and therefore refuse further loans. The SFP also shows the liquidity position of a business. By looking at the level of current assets and current liabilities it is easy to assess whether a business is liquid- i.e. does it have sufficient current assets to pay its bills as they fall due.

(4) Comparing the SPL and SFP

Similarities:

Both the SFP and SPL are produced for external users (usually once a year). They are both prepared using the accruals/matching concept and the going concern concept.

An example of the accruals concept would be telephone expense incurred but not paid would be shown as an expense in the SPL. The amount not paid would be shown as an accrual in the SFP.

The going concern concept also assumes that the business will continue to trade for the foreseeable future.

Finally both the SPL and SFP will be prepared under accounting standards. For example IAS 16 Property, plant and equipment.

Differences

The SFP is showing the assets/liabilities/capital position on one day only i.e. the end of the year.

By contrast the SPL shows the results of the business over the last 12 months (i.e. all the revenue/income and expenses from Jan to December).

Advantages

As mentioned above the SPL and SFP provide useful information to the users of accounts which they will then use to make decisions. These decisions include for investors, whether to invest in a business, for banks whether to lend money to the business. For suppliers, whether to offer credit terms to a business.

Disadvantages

Both the SPF and SPL report on past performance i.e. on results already happened and this may not be a reflection of what will happen in the future.

The accounts are prepared under accounting standards and this often involves a choice i.e. straight line and reducing balance depreciation and this could perhaps lead to manipulation of the accounts.

The SFP also shows the cash position at the year-end but does not explain exactly where this cash has come from or what it has been spent on.

The SFP also shows some items at historical cost i.e. land may be shown in the accounts at the amount paid, not the amount it is currently worth.

The SFP also does not show any internally generated assets such as the goodwill/ reputation of the business.

71 CASH

THREE reasons why the net profit of a business for a period is not necessarily the same as the net cash generated in the same period.

Reason 1 – Timing differences

Timing difference are when the same figure eventually affects both profit and cash to the same degree but the timing is different.

Examples

- If sales of £1,000 are made in a month, then we expect to receive £1,000 cash but the customer may not pay for some months afterwards due to being given a credit period. The difference between sales and cash will be via receivables.

- Similarly if items of inventory are purchased, then the cost only impacts profit when the items are sold. If still in the warehouse, then the cost gets carried forward as closing inventory. The cash will be paid after receiving an invoice and waiting a given credit period.

Reason 2 – Items that affect profit but have no cash impact

Some items affect profit but do not have a cash implication.

Examples

- Depreciation reduces profit but is not a cash flow. (The long term cash equivalent would relate to buying/selling assets.)

- Another example would be making a provision for doubtful debts – these are recognised as an expense in the profit and loss account but the other side of the double entry is to reduce the receivables balance in the statement of financial position. There is no cash impact.

Reason 3 – Items that affect cash but do not affect profit

Finally, some items impact cash but do not go through the profit and loss account and do not affect profit.

Examples

- Owners taking drawings out of the business would reduce cash but are seen as an appropriation of profit rather than an expense.

- Similarly, payment of a dividend may reduce cash and use up retained profits but does not affect net profit for the period.

- Taking out or repaying a loan will impact cash but the other side of the double entry is on the statement of financial position not the profit and loss account.

---

72 CYCLE

(a) Mthbe needs to keep up-to-date in the following areas (only TWO needed):

- tax legislation/compliance

- money laundering regulations

- accounting/reporting standards

- regulation of accounting.

The reasons for this are as follows:

- They are important areas because clients are businesses, which must comply with requirement for accurate accounts preparation and tax returns.

- Mthbe needs to ensure he is technically competent to undertake the work (fundamental principle of professional competence and due care).

- Mthbe needs to protect himself re money laundering.

(b) The AAT CPD policy asks Mthbe to update his skills twice a year.

(c) The AAT's CPD cycle has four stages – assess, plan, action and evaluation.

73 SARAH

(a) Sarah should obtain authority from the client to give the financial information.

(b) It is not possible to give an assurance regarding the client ability to pay the rent.

74 ADAM

Matter 1

Adam is obliged to report this refusal to disclose and the information surrounding it to the firm's Money Laundering Reporting Officer (MLRO).

Matter 2

This scenario also gives grounds for suspicion of money laundering. Why doesn't the client, H Ltd, simply want LOFT to repay them and then it up to them whether they want to pay anything to Q Ltd? Is it to make funds difficult to trace, so 'dirty cash' becomes a nice clean cheque from a reputable accounting firm?

Any overpayment by a customer should be thoroughly investigated by a senior member of finance function staff and only repaid to the customer once it has been established that it is right/legal to do so.

Similarly the request to pay a third party should be scrutinised before any payment is agreed to. Without further information the transaction does not make commercial sense.

Unless investigations satisfy any concerns raised, then LOFT should refuse the payment and the MRLO should fill in a Suspicious Activity Report (SAR) to be sent to the NCA (previously known as SOCA).

MMAC

TASK 1.5

Assessment objective 4	Use relevant spreadsheet skills to analyse, interpret and report management accounting data

75 ALLOCATION AND APPORTION

Overhead cost	Basis	Mending £	Stores £	Canteen £	Total £
Specific overheads	Allocate	4,000	1,000	2,000	7,000
Rent	Floor space	16,000	10,000	4,000	30,000
Building maintenance	Floor space	24,000	15,000	6,000	45,000
Machinery insurance	Value of machinery	1,344	1,056	0	2,400
Machinery depreciation	Value of machinery	6,160	4,840	0	11,000
Machinery running cost	Machinery hours	3,750	2,250	0	6,000
Power	Power usage	5,600	700	700	7,000
Total		60,854	34,846	12,700	108,400

76 REAPPORTIONMENT

Overhead cost	Basis	Mending £	Stores £	Canteen £	Total £
Sub-Total		60,854	34,846	12,700	108,400
Re-apportion Canteen	Number of employees	9,525	3,175	(12,700)	
Re-apportion Stores	Value of stores requisitions	38,021	(38,021)		
Total		108,400			108,400

77 PACKAGING

	Flexed Budget	Actual	Variance	Favourable F or Adverse A
Volume sold	259,200	259,200		
	£000	£000	£000	
Sales revenue	3,600 ÷ 180 × 259.2 = 5,184	6,480	1,296	F
Less costs:				
Direct materials	630 ÷ 180 × 259.2 = 907	954	47	A
Direct labour	720 ÷ 180 × 259.2 = 1,037	864	173	F
Overheads	(fixed) 1,764	2,210	446	A
Operating profit	5,184 − (907 + 1,037 + 1,764) = 1,476	2,452	976	F

78 LF

Task 1

	X	Y	Z
Total sales (£)	1,000,000	1,125,000	625,000
Total variable cost (£)	(750,000)	(750,000)	(500,000)
Total contribution (£)	250,000	375,000	125,000
Units sold	5,000	7,500	2,500
Contribution per unit	£50	£50	£50
Machine hours per unit	20	21	26
Contribution per machine hour	£2.50	£2.38	£1.92
Rank	1	2	3

Task 2

Production Plan

Product	Units	Hours used
X	5,000	100,000
Y	7,500	157,500
Z	39,000 ÷ 26 = 1,500	39,000
Total hours available		296,500

Task 3

Product	Units	Contribution per unit	Total contribution £
X	5,000	£50	250,000
Y	7,500	£50	375,000
Z	1,500	£50	75,000
			700,000
Fixed costs (200,000 + 315,000 + 130,000)			(645,000)
Total profit			55,000

79 HEATH

(a) $\dfrac{17,150}{19-12} = 2,450 \text{ units}$

(b) $\dfrac{17,150}{7/19} = £46,550$

Or $2,450 \times 19 = £46,550$

(c)

Units of H sold	4,000	5,000
Margin of safety (units)	4,000 − 2,450 = 1,550 units	5,000 − 2,450 = 2,550 units
Margin of safety percentage	$\dfrac{4,000-2,450}{4,000}\times100 = 38.75\%$	$\dfrac{5,000-2,450}{5,000}\times100 = 51\%$

(d) $\dfrac{17,150 + 24,850}{7} = 6,000 \text{ units}$

(e) The correct answer is **B** – an increase in selling price means that contribution per unit increases therefore fewer units have to be made to cover the fixed costs. If BEP is lower than the margin of safety is higher.

80   BLINDS

(a)   **Net present value**

	Year 0 £000	Year 1 £000	Year 2 £000	Year 3 £000
Capital expenditure	−547			
Sales income		290	340	400
Operating costs		−120	−120	−120
Net cash flows	−547	170	220	280
PV factors	1.0000	0.909	0.826	0.751
Discounted cash flows	−547	155	182	210
Net present value	0			

(b)   **Payback period**

Year	Cash flow £000	Cumulative cash flow £000
0	(547)	(547)
1	170	(377)
2	220	(157)
3	280	123

The payback period is **2** years and **7** months.

Months = 157/280 × 12 = 6.7 months.

(c)   If the NPV of a project is nil then the cost of capital equals the Internal Rate of Return (IRR).

True

(d)   If the IRR of an investment is higher than the company's cost of capital then the investment should go ahead.

True

ANSWERS TO EXAM – PART II PRACTICE TASKS

The answers to the tasks in the scenarios can be found on MyKaplan account in AVSY Exam Kit: Scenarios Excel Data & Answers.

Please go to www.mykaplan.co.uk and login to the AVSY section.

Section 5

MOCK ASSESSMENT – QUESTIONS

PART 1

TASK 1.1 (15 marks)

This task is based on a workplace scenario separate to the rest of the assessment.

An accountant, Siobahn, has recently started work at Plug Ltd, a large organisation with many employees. She mainly works in the accounts department and is currently responsible for performing bank reconciliations and control account reconciliations. She is trying to apply the ethical code's conceptual framework to some ethical problems she is facing at work and is currently evaluating threats to her fundamental principles.

(a) **Are these statements true or false?** (2 marks)

Statement	True	False
The AAT code of ethics gives detailed rules that cover a wide range of possible scenarios.		✓
Some of the ethical principles can be overlooked if it is in the public interest to do so.	✓	

(b) **For each of the following scenarios identify the nature of the ethical threat.** (2 marks)

Scenario	Threat
Siobahn is seconded to internal audit and asked to verify that control procedures have been followed correctly, including bank reconciliations.	✓
Siobahn's brother is one of Plug Ltd's suppliers.	✓

∇ Drop down list for task 1.1 (b)

Self-interest threat	
Self-review threat	✓
Advocacy threat	
Familiarity threat	✓
Intimidation threat	

An ex-boyfriend of Siobahn is demanding that she reveal confidential information about Plug Ltd's manufacturing processes or he will publish compromising photographs of her online.

(c)   Identify whether the following statements are true or false.   **(3 marks)**

Statement	True	False
Siobahn may never disclose confidential information to any third party.		✓
The threat that Siobahn is facing to her compliance with the fundamental principles is a self-interest threat.		✓
Siobahn must resign immediately from Plug Ltd as her integrity has been compromised by her past relationships.		✓

Terry is also an accountant as Plug Ltd and often helps the sales department when pitching for new contracts. Whilst pitching for a contract in the local area, Plug Ltd was competing against the main rival local firm. The competitor firm is in serious financial difficulties and approached Terry to offer him an all-expenses paid holiday in return for offering a more expensive price to the potential client. It turns out that the competitor would have gone into administration without this contract win. James has been unsure as to whether he should accept the offer.

(d)   Complete the following statement.   **(2 marks)**

Being offered gifts by the rival firm is [▽   ] to Terry's fundamental

principle of [▽   ]

▽ Drop down list for task 1.1 (d)

a self-interest threat   ✓
a familiarity threat
objectivity   ✓
professional competence

Terry has decided not to accept the holiday and inflate his recommended price, despite his belief that Plug Ltd was unlikely to win the tender anyway.

(e)   Identify whether the following statements are true or false.   **(3 marks)**

Statement	True	False
Had he accepted the holiday, Terry would have been guilty of the offence of 'active' bribery under the UK Bribery Act (2010).		✓
The UK Bribery Act (2010) only applies to UK citizens, residents and companies established under UK law.		✓
Not all gifts or hospitality would be considered to be bribes.	✓	

Recently Bath plc, a customer of Plug Ltd, sent in a cheque for £80,000 in payment of an invoice for £8,000. When Terry queried this, the client said it was a mistake and asked for a cheque for the difference of £72,000 to be written to Faucet plc, a sister company of Bath plc.

(f) **Identify whether the following statements are true or false.** **(3 marks)**

Statement	True	False
Terry should report the matter to the firm's MRLO.	✓	
Plug Ltd should scrutinise the request carefully before agreeing to any payment.	✓	
Unless investigations satisfy any concerns raised, then the MRLO should fill in a Suspicious Activity Report (SAR) to be sent to the NCA.	✓	

TASK 1.2 (15 marks)

This task is based on the workplace scenario of Ovey and Sach.

Today's date is 1 March 20X6

Ovey and Sach's VAT account at 30 September, the end of its last VAT period, is as follows:

		£			£
		500	30/06	Balance b/d	4,561.02
30/09	Purchases day book	4,532.25	30/09	Sales day book	5,587.32
30/09	Sales returns day book	785.69	30/09	Purchases returns day book	403.68
30/09	Balance c/d	5,234.08			
		10,552.02			10,552.02

On reviewing Ovey and Sach's day books, you have found two errors:

- Input VAT of £56.50 on a purchases invoice was wrongly recorded as purchases on 29 July.

- A sales invoice for a zero rated supply of £500 (net) had been entered twice in the sales day book.

You prepare journals to correct these errors.

(a) **Once the journals have been processed, what will be the revised balance carried down on the VAT account?** **(2 marks)**

£	

(b) **Complete the following sentence by selecting ONE of the options below.** **(1 mark)**

This balance will appear on the _____ side of the trial balance.

Credit	✓
Debit	

It is now 14 October. You have just received an invoice from Briggs Ltd where the VAT has been incorrectly calculated. You rang the supplier to query this and were told that your colleague, Graham Hyde, was aware of this and always agreed to the invoices before.

You suspect that your colleague is involved in fraud and possibly even money laundering but are not sure what best to do next.

(c) **Which of the following options describes what you should do next?** **(2 marks)**

Confront Graham with your suspicions	
Discuss the matter with Susan Wright, the chief accountant	✓
Call the police	
Resign	

It is a week later and you are now very suspicious that Graham is involved in money laundering so decide to send a Suspicious Activity Report to the National Crime Agency. Over lunch the next day you boast to him that his fraudulent behaviour is about to be stopped as you have reported him.

(d) **What offence are you potentially guilty of here?** **(2 marks)**

None – you have done nothing wrong	
A breach of confidentiality	
Money laundering	
Tipping off	✓

Mike Ovey and Andrew Sach are worried whether there are other issues relating to the recording of purchases and amounts owed to suppliers. As a result of this, they ask you to perform a logic check of purchase ledger transactions for the month of September 20X6.

Using as many verified figures as possible, such as confirmed balances from suppliers, you construct the following purchase ledger control account:

Purchases ledger control account

	£		£
		Balance b/d	14,875
		Purchases day book	4,256
Contra	100		
Cash book	2,365		
Balance c/d	15,977		
Total		**Total**	

(e) **Calculate the missing figure in the purchases ledger control account.** **(2 marks)**

£ 689

(f) **Which of the following could the missing figure represent?** **(2 marks)**

Overstated purchase invoices	✓
Understated purchase invoices	

You undertake a similar exercise with respect to sales and discover that some customers are being given discounts that they do not deserve and have not been authorised. You raise the issue with the clerk concerned who tells you to "mind your own business or there could be trouble".

(g) **Applying the conceptual framework from the ethical code, which ONE of the following describes the situation faced by you?** **(2 marks)**

A self-review threat to professional competence and due care.	
An intimidation threat to objectivity.	✓
A familiarity threat to professional behaviour.	

In response to this threat you decide to call the AAT ethics helpline and discuss the invoices concerned for advice.

(h) **Complete the following statement by selecting ONE of the options below.** **(2 marks)**

In relation to the evidence and documents, the accountant must be particularly careful to ensure the fundamental principle of _____ is not breached when seeking guidance.

confidentiality	✓
professional competence and due care	
professional behaviour	

TASK 1.3 (15 marks)

This task is based on the workplace scenario of Ovey and Sach.

You are Tina Jeffrey, a part-qualified Accounting Technician. You work for Ovey and Sach, a business which makes and sells designer gifts. Ovey and Sach is a partnership owned by Mike Ovey and Andrew Sach.

Today's date is 31 March 20X8.

Mike Ovey and Andrew Sach have decided to raise additional finance to increase the product range and grow the business. As part of a loan application they need to produce a report for the bank. Unfortunately Susan Wright is currently off sick and Andrew Sach has told you to produce the report.

The deadline suggested appears unrealistic, especially given the complexity of the work.

You feel that you are not sufficiently experienced to complete the work alone but your manager appears unable to offer the necessary support. You feel slightly intimidated by Andrew Sachs, and also feel under pressure to be a 'team player' and help out. However, if you try to complete the work to the required quality but fail, you could be subject to criticism and other repercussions.

(a) **Explain TWO threats to your ethical principles from Andrew Sach's request, and explain what actions you should take next. In your answer you should refer to the guidance found in the ethical code for professional accountants.** **(6 marks)**

Threat 1

***

Threat 2

***

Actions I should take

***

You receive the following email from Andrew Sach:

To: Tina Jeffrey

From: Andrew Sach

Date: 5/4/X8

Hello Tina

We have decided to delay completing the loan application until Susan is back with us as we feel it is vital that we get this right. Obviously we would still appreciate your input but want Susan to check everything before it goes to the bank.

In preliminary discussions with the bank I got the distinct impression that they would consider our application more favourably if we became a limited company rather than remain the partnership we currently operate as. I must confess to being confused and am now wondering whether we should be trying to raise new equity finance.

I would like you to tell me more about the implications of a partnership becoming a limited company as far as finance is concerned.

Please include three sections in your response to me as follows:

(1)   A brief description of a limited company and how switching could change the liability faced by Mike Ovey and myself.

(2)   Three reasons why the bank may prefer to lend to companies rather than partnerships.

(3)   The difference in the way companies can raise equity finance compared to a partnership.

Regards,
Andrew

(b)   Reply to Andrew, addressing all three points that he has raised.   **(10 marks)**

To:	Andrew Sachs
From:	Tina Jeffrey
Date:	5/4/X8

Subject:

(1)

(2)

(3)

PART 2

You will be required to open an **Excel spreadsheet** called **Laura** that contains data you require for this assessment. The spreadsheet can be found on MyKaplan. The spreadsheet will need to be downloaded and saved before starting the tasks.

You MUST save your work at regular intervals during this assessment to prevent you losing work.

TASK 2.1   (25 marks)

Laura's Luggage manufactures and sells luggage to retailers, online and through their own 'Factory' outlet.

The company wish to work out how well the '**Luxury**' brand of luggage has been performing in the online sales and have asked you to assist them by building a spreadsheet to help them calculate costs, revenue and profits for 20X4.

You have been asked to use the information below to prepare documents to show how the business has performed in the last twelve months.

Month	Opening inventory	Production volume	Sales volume
January	11,236	32,375	24,998
February		40,400	42,016
March		36,360	39,996
April		58,075	46,000
May		38,250	42,075
June		71,775	77,517
July		73,800	81,180
August		56,250	60,750
September		39,000	37,400
October		48,000	48,960
November		60,000	56,345
December		70,000	71,400

This data is given you in the sheet "volumes" in the Laura Workbook.

The table below shows the way in which the company calculated cost and sales prices during 20X4.

Quarter	Production cost	Sales price
Qtr 1	£48.50	Cost + 23%
Qtr 2	4%	Cost + 23%
Qtr 3	6%	Cost + 23%
Qtr 4	5%	Cost + 25%

(a)   Open a new workbook. Name the file as 'your surname, initial and assessment date (yyyymmdd)' and save the file. Insert a footer on every worksheet in the workbook with your full name and AAT student number in the left hand pane.

(b)   Open a new worksheet. Starting in Cell A5 input the monthly figures for opening inventory, production volumes and sales volumes in adjacent columns and create titles for the columns.

(c)   Insert a column after the sales volume column and call this closing inventory.

(d)   Use formulae to calculate the following:

- The closing inventory for each month (closing inventory is calculated as opening Inventory plus production volume minus sales volume).

- The opening inventory for each month by bringing forward the closing volume from the previous month.

- The total production volumes for 20X4 and the total sales volume for 20X4.

(e)   Format the your table of data in the following way:

- The figures in your table of data should be set to number to 0 decimal places with a 1000 separator.

- The column headings, using bold, Arial, font size 11 and wrapped over 2 lines to reduce column width.

- Totals should be in bold.

(f)   Insert the title 'Production and Sales Volumes 20X4', in the top row of your worksheet as bold, Arial and font size 14. The title should be merged and centred across the table of data and underlined.

(g)   In Row 23 you are going to create a second table of data that converts all the volumes from the table above into monetary figures.

1   Copy the column and row headings into the new table at Row 23.

2   Alter the column headings to Month, Opening Inventory, Variable Costs, Sales Revenue and Closing Inventory.

3   Use the table of quarterly production costs and sales prices (above) and convert the volumes to monetary values.

- Closing inventory figures should still be brought forward.

- Closing inventory should be valued at the production cost for the quarter.

- The increase in production costs are a percentage increase from Quarter 1.

4   Total all the columns.

(h)   You are now required to use formulae to calculate Gross and Net Profit figures. To do this you will need to do the following:

    1   Next to the closing inventory column create a column for Cost of Sales. As this is a manufacturing accounting-system, Cost of Sales is calculated as 'Opening Inventory plus Variable Costs minus closing inventory'.

    2   Alongside Cost of Sales create a column for Gross Profit. Gross Profit is calculated as 'Sales Revenue minus Cost of Sales.

    3   Alongside Gross Profit create a column for Expenses. Expenses are £63,000 in Quarter 1 rising by 5% in each successive quarter.

    4   Alongside Expenses create a column for Net Profit. Net Profit is calculated as 'Gross Profit minus Expenses'.

    5   Total all the columns.

(i)   Alongside the Net Profit column create two more columns for Gross Profit Margin and Net Profit Margin.

    1   Gross Profit margin is Gross Profit as a percentage of Sales Revenue.

    2   Net Profit margin is Net Profit as a percentage of Sales Revenue.

    3   Calculate average Gross and Net Profit margins (average margins are calculated by expressing total gross/net profit as a percentage of total sales).

(j)   Two rows above the table insert the title Profits and Margins for 20X4.

    1   The title should be in bold, underlined and Arial font size 14.

    2   The title should be merged and centred across all the columns.

(k)   Format the table in the following way:

    1   Make sure that all the above columns are suitably labelled.

    2   Wrap text in the columns so that the columns are a suitable width.

    3   All column headers should be in **bold**.

    4   All column totals should be in **bold**.

    5   Format all monetary cells to currency to two decimal places.

    6   Percentages should be to two decimal places.

    7   Average margin figures should be **bold** and cell fill should be yellow.

    8   Name the worksheet Lugg001.

(l)   Copy Lugg001 to a new worksheet and show formulas. Adjust column widths so the data fits neatly in the columns. Name this worksheet Lugg001(F).

(m)   Prepare Lugg001 and Lugg001(F) so that they would print to 1 × A4 page if required. Choose the most suitable page orientation.

TASK 2.2   **(30 marks)**

You have been asked to investigate different aspects of the budget for 20X4.

Firstly, you need to review the variable costs for the first quarter of 20X4 (January, February and March) which were entered onto the computer by your line manager. This information is in the Laura Workbook labelled as 'VCosts 20X4' in the Laura Workbook.

(a)   Unprotect the worksheet using VC20X4 as the password. Open a new worksheet in your workbook and copy only the relevant information from the 'VCosts20X4' worksheet. Replace the title with 'Variable Costs Quarter 1 20X4' using Arial font in size 14 in a merged cell (left aligned) over all the data columns. The title should be in bold, underlined and in Italics.

(b)   Format the column headers with bold text ensuring column widths and row heights are suitable for the contents. Wrap text across 2 lines.

(c)   Format all the dates as dd/mm/yyyy, make amendments as required so that all dates are in the required format. Sort the data by date, in ascending order, ensuring only the correct information is used for the quarter.

(d)   You have discovered additional Direct Materials and Variable Overheads not included in the spreadsheet. Insert rows and/or columns at the correct date and enter the following costs. Ensure the row total calculates correctly and it must remain as the last column on the worksheet.

- Direct Materials 7th February   £112,077.80
- Direct Materials 16 Jan 14   £179,440.10
- 5th Jan, Variable Overheads   £14,800
- 5th Feb, Variable Overheads   £12,300
- 5th March, Variable Overheads   £11,100

(e)   Total all the columns and then use functions to calculate the average and median Direct Material costs ensuring the cells containing the functions are clearly labelled. These labels should be in **bold**. Ensure the format of all numerical cells is currency rounded to two decimal places.

(f)   Use conditional formatting to highlight cells in which the Direct Materials values exceed the average figure for Direct Materials by 10%. The conditional formatting should change the cell fill to Red and the text to white and bold.

(g)   Produce a Pie Chart of the column totals. Insert the chart to the right of the variable costs data table. Ensure the legend contains the column header names and that the chart has a suitable title. The Pie Chart should show percentages.

(h)   Name this worksheet tab 'Quarter 1 VarCosts' and ensure all of the information is displayed in a way that could be printed on one A4 page. Save this worksheet.

Secondly, the managers have some queries concerning bag sales.

Laura's Luggage sells a range of ladies bags. All sales have been recorded on the 'LLData' worksheet in the Laura Workbook. Copy the data from this worksheet into a new worksheet in your workbook.

You have been asked to identify the most popular type of bag sold and the best performing sales method, (Internet, Factory Shop or Retail) from this information of each type of sale.

You need to create pivot table(s) from this information to identify the most popular ladies bag by value and the value of the sales for each outlet.

(i)   Check the data table to ensure there is nothing to prevent pivot tables from working. Make any changes you feel necessary to update the table (do not alter any values).

(j)   There has been an error in inputting; Internet sales have been recorded both as 'Internet' and 'Online'. Replace all instances of 'Online' with 'Internet'.

(k)   Create a pivot table with an appropriate heading. The pivot table should be placed to the right of the data set. Use the pivot table to identify the most popular type of bag sold by value and sales outlet. Identify the bag that generates the highest income by colouring the font of the highest income figures red.

(l)   Create another pivot table with an appropriate heading to show total sales by sales outlet (Internet, Factory Shop or Retail), indicating which one of the three outlets generates the most income. You may need to update the data in some way to allow this to be done.

(m)   Colour the font of the highest income figure red and arrange the figures of the pivot table in descending order. Name the tab 'Bags' and remember to save your work.

Section 6

MOCK ASSESSMENT – ANSWERS

PART 1

TASK 1.1 (15 marks)

(a) **Are these statements true or false?** (2 marks)

Statement	True	False
The AAT code of ethics gives detailed rules that cover a wide range of possible scenarios.		✓
Some of the ethical principles can be overlooked if it is in the public interest to do so.	✓	

Note:

1   The code gives principles rather than rules.

2   An example of this would be whistleblowing, where confidentiality is breached.

(b) **For each of the following scenarios identify the nature of the ethical threat.** (2 marks)

Scenario	Threat
Siobahn is seconded to internal audit and asked to verify that control procedures have been followed correctly, including bank reconciliations.	Self-review threat
Siobahn's brother is one of Plug Ltd's suppliers.	Familiarity threat

(c) **Identify whether the following statements are true or false.** (3 marks)

Statement	True	False
Siobahn may never disclose confidential information to any third party.		✓
The threat that Siobahn is facing to her compliance with the fundamental principles is a self-interest threat.		✓
Siobahn must resign immediately from Plug Ltd as her integrity has been compromised by her past relationships.		✓

Note:

1   Siobahn may disclose information if given permission to do so.

2   This is an example of an intimidation threat.

3   Siobahn should discuss the matter with her manager and possibly even with the police.

(d) **Complete the following statement.** **(2 marks)**

Being offered gifts by the rival firm is | a self-interest threat | to Terry's fundamental principle of | objectivity |

(e) **Identify whether the following statements are true or false.** **(3 marks)**

Statement	True	False
Had he accepted the holiday, Terry would have been guilty of the offence of 'active' bribery under the UK Bribery Act (2010).		✓
The UK Bribery Act (2010) only applies to UK citizens, residents and companies established under UK law.		✓
Not all gifts or hospitality would be considered to be bribes.	✓	

Note:

1   Terry would have been guilty of "passive" bribery – receiving a bribe.

2   The UK Act also applies to.

3   Very small gifts or acts of hospitality would not be considered bribes.

(f) **Identify whether the following statements are true or false.** **(3 marks)**

Statement	True	False
Terry should report the matter to the firm's MRLO.	✓	
Plug Ltd should scrutinise the request carefully before agreeing to any payment.	✓	
Unless investigations satisfy any concerns raised, then the MRLO should fill in a Suspicious Activity Report (SAR) to be sent to the NCA.	✓	

Note:

There is a strong suspicion of money laundering in these circumstances.

TASK 1.2 (15 marks)

(a) **Once the journals have been processed, what will be the revised balance carried down on the VAT account?** **(2 marks)**

£	5,177.58

Input VAT should be £56.50 higher, so the balance should be 5,234.08 – 56.50.

The zero rated sales invoice will not affect the VAT balance.

(b) **Complete the following sentence by selecting ONE of the options below.** **(1 mark)**

This balance will appear on the _____ side of the trial balance.

Credit	✓
Debit	

(c)   **Which of the following options describes what you should do next?**   **(2 marks)**

Confront Graham with your suspicions	
Discuss the matter with Susan Wright, the chief accountant	✓
Call the police	
Resign	

(d)   **What offence are you potentially guilty of here?**   **(2 marks)**

None – you have done nothing wrong	
A breach of confidentiality	
Money laundering	
Tipping off	✓

(e)   **Calculate the missing figure in the purchases ledger control account.**   **(1 mark)**

£	689

Purchases ledger control account

	£		£
		Balance b/d	14,875
		Purchases day book	4,256
Contra	100		
Cash book	2,365		
Balance c/d	15,977		
Difference	689		
Total	19,131	**Total**	19,131

(f)   **Which of the following could the missing figure represent?**   **(2 marks)**

Overstated purchase invoices	✓
Understated purchase invoices	

Given the difference is on the debit side, then one cause could be the credit side being too high – the PDB figure is overstated.

(g)   **Applying the conceptual framework from the ethical code, which ONE of the following describes the situation faced by you?**   **(2 marks)**

A self-review threat to professional competence and due care.	
An intimidation threat to objectivity.	✓
A familiarity threat to professional behaviour.	

(h) **Complete the following statement by selecting ONE of the options below.** **(2 marks)**

In relation to the evidence and documents, the accountant must be particularly careful to ensure the fundamental principle of _____ is not breached when seeking guidance.

confidentiality	✓
professional competence and due care	
professional behaviour	

TASK 1.3 **(15 marks)**

(a) **Threat 1**

> **Professional competence and due care:**
>
> It would not be right for me to attempt to complete work that is technically beyond my abilities without proper supervision.
>
> This is made worse by my concern whether it is even possible to complete the work within the time available and still act diligently to achieve the required quality of output.

Threat 2

> **Objectivity:**
>
> Pressure from Andrew Sach, combined with the fear of repercussions, gives rise to an intimidation threat to my objectivity.
>
> If the loan application is unsuccessful then there is also the possibility that will impact other people's jobs, again adding to threat to objectivity.

Actions I should take

> I should use the Conceptual Framework to apply relevant safeguards to bring the threat to my principles down to an acceptable level OR I should use the ethical conflict resolution process stated in the code. I should follow any internal procedure for reporting/dealing with such threats.
>
> I should discuss my concerns with Andrew Sachs that I do not have sufficient time and experience to complete the work to a satisfactory standard and suggest how the problem may be resolved. For example, the use of a subcontract accountant or the possibility of assigning another member of staff to supervise my work.
>
> If I am still under pressure to do the work, then I should get advice from the AAT and as to what to do next.
>
> It would be unethical to attempt to complete the work if I doubt my competence.

(b)   **Reply to Andrew, addressing all three points that he has raised.**   **(10 marks)**

To:	Andrew Sachs
From:	Tina Jeffrey
Date:	5/4/X8

Subject:	Raising finance

(1)   **Limited companies**

A limited company is an organisation that is a separate legal entity distinct from its owners (unlike a partnership or sole trader). The ownership of a company is through share ownership.

At present Mike Ovey and yourself have unlimited personal liability for partnership debts. With a "limited" company the liability of owners (shareholders) is limited to any unpaid amounts on shares purchased. Thus, for example, the bank would not be able to pursue Mike Ovey and yourself if the business struggled to repay the loan.

For this reason, some banks may insist on personal guarantees from the owners, separate from the company.

(2)   **Bank loans**

Banks may prefer to lend to companies for the following reasons:

    (1)   A limited company must prepare annual accounts (also known as 'statutory accounts') from the company's records at the end of the financial year. Partners are not legally required to produce annual accounts or file accounts for inspection.

    (2)   Larger companies' financial statements must be audited, possibly making them more reliable and accurate.

    (3)   A company's accounts must be prepared in accordance with the Companies Act 2006, possibly making it easier to assess the business' performance.

(3)   **Equity finance**

Companies can raise equity finance by issuing new shares to investors.

With partnerships, either the existing partners could introduce further capital or a new partner could be admitted. Introducing new partners would involve having to change the partnership agreement.

PART 2

TASK 2.1

Production and Sales volumes 20X4			
Month	Opening inventory	Production volume	Sales volume	Closing inventory
January	11,236	32,375	24,998	18,613
February	18,613	40,400	42,016	16,997
March	16,997	36,360	39,996	13,361
April	13,361	58,075	46,000	25,436
May	25,436	38,250	42,075	21,611
June	21,611	71,775	77,517	15,869
July	15,869	73,800	81,180	8,489
August	8,489	56,250	60,750	3,989
September	3,989	39,000	37,400	5,589
October	5,589	48,000	48,960	4,629
November	4,629	60,000	56,345	8,284
December	8,284	70,000	71,400	6,884
		624,285	628,637	

Month	Opening inventory	Production volume	Sales volume	Closing inventory
January	11236	32375	24998	=B5+C5-D5
February	=E5	40400	42016	=B6+C6-D6
March	=E6	36360	39996	=B7+C7-D7
April	=E7	58075	46000	=B8+C8-D8
May	=E8	38250	42075	=B9+C9-D9
June	=E9	71775	77517	=B10+C10-D10
July	=E10	73800	81180	=B11+C11-D11
August	=E11	56250	60750	=B12+C12-D12
September	=E12	39000	37400	=B13+C13-D13
October	=E13	48000	48960	=B14+C14-D14
November	=E14	60000	56345	=B15+C15-D15
December	=E15	70000	71400	=B16+C16-D16
		=SUM(C5:C16)	=SUM(D5:D16)	

Profits and Margins for 20X4

Month	Opening Inventory	Variable Costs	Sales Revenue	Closing Inventory	Cost of Sales	Gross Profit	Expenses	Net Profit	Gross Profit Margin	Net Profit Margin
January	£544,946.00	£1,570,187.50	£1,491,380.68	£902,730.50	£1,212,403.00	£278,977.68	£63,000.00	£215,977.68	18.71%	14.48%
February	£902,730.50	£1,959,400.00	£2,506,674.56	£824,354.50	£2,037,776.00	£468,898.56	£63,000.00	£405,898.56	18.71%	16.19%
March	£824,354.50	£1,763,460.00	£2,386,161.36	£648,008.50	£1,939,806.00	£446,355.36	£63,000.00	£383,355.36	18.71%	16.07%
April	£648,008.50	£2,929,303.00	£2,853,840.00	£1,282,991.84	£2,294,319.66	£559,520.34	£66,150.00	£493,370.34	19.61%	17.29%
May	£1,282,991.84	£1,929,330.00	£2,610,333.00	£1,090,058.84	£2,122,263.00	£488,070.00	£66,150.00	£421,920.00	18.70%	16.16%
June	£1,090,058.84	£3,620,331.00	£4,809,154.68	£800,432.36	£3,909,957.48	£899,197.20	£66,150.00	£833,047.20	18.70%	17.32%
July	£800,432.36	£3,794,058.00	£5,133,011.40	£436,419.49	£4,158,070.87	£974,940.53	£69,457.50	£905,483.03	18.99%	17.64%
August	£436,419.49	£2,891,812.50	£3,841,222.50	£205,074.49	£3,123,157.50	£718,065.00	£69,457.50	£648,607.50	18.69%	16.89%
September	£205,074.49	£2,004,990.00	£2,364,802.00	£287,330.49	£1,922,734.00	£442,068.00	£69,457.50	£372,610.50	18.69%	15.76%
October	£287,330.49	£2,444,640.00	£3,116,793.60	£235,754.97	£2,496,215.52	£620,578.08	£72,930.38	£547,647.71	19.91%	17.57%
November	£235,754.97	£3,055,800.00	£3,586,922.70	£421,904.12	£2,869,650.85	£717,271.85	£72,930.38	£644,341.48	20.00%	17.96%
December	£421,904.12	£3,565,100.00	£4,545,324.00	£350,602.12	£3,636,402.00	£908,922.00	£72,930.38	£835,991.63	20.00%	18.39%
	£7,680,006.10	£31,528,412.00	£39,245,620.48	£7,485,662.22	£31,722,755.88	£7,522,864.60	£814,613.63	£6,708,250.98	19.17%	17.09%

This table has been included here to show where the numbers have come from for the calculation of variable costs, sales revenue and closing inventory.

Quarter	Production Cost	Sales Price
Qtr 1	£48.50	£59.66
Qtr 2	£50.44	£62.04
Qtr 3	£51.41	£63.23
Qtr 4	£50.93	£63.66

Profits and Margins for 20X4

Month	Opening Inventory	Variable Costs	Sales Revenue	Closing Inventory	Cost of Sales	Gross Profit	Expenses	Net Profit	Gross Profit Margin	Net Profit Margin
January	=B5*48.5	=C5*48.5	=D5*59.66	=E5*48.5	=B24+C24-E24	=D24-F24	63000	=G24-H24	=G24/D24	=I24/D24
February	=E24	=C6*48.5	=D6*59.66	=E6*48.5	=B25+C25-E25	=D25-F25	63000	=G25-H25	=G25/D25	=I25/D25
March	=E25	=C7*48.5	=D7*59.66	=E7*48.5	=B26+C26-E26	=D26-F26	63000	=G26-H26	=G26/D26	=I26/D26
April	=E26	=C8*50.44	=D8*62.04	=E8*50.44	=B27+C27-E27	=D27-F27	=$H$26*1.05	=G27-H27	=G27/D27	=I27/D27
May	=E27	=C9*50.44	=D9*62.04	=E9*50.44	=B28+C28-E28	=D28-F28	=$H$26*1.05	=G28-H28	=G28/D28	=I28/D28
June	=E28	=C10*50.44	=D10*62.04	=E10*50.44	=B29+C29-E29	=D29-F29	=$H$26*1.05	=G29-H29	=G29/D29	=I29/D29
July	=E29	=C11*51.41	=D11*63.23	=E11*51.41	=B30+C30-E30	=D30-F30	=$H$29*1.05	=G30-H30	=G30/D30	=I30/D30
August	=E30	=C12*51.41	=D12*63.23	=E12*51.41	=B31+C31-E31	=D31-F31	=$H$29*1.05	=G31-H31	=G31/D31	=I31/D31
September	=E31	=C13*51.41	=D13*63.23	=E13*51.41	=B32+C32-E32	=D32-F32	=$H$29*1.05	=G32-H32	=G32/D32	=I32/D32
October	=E32	=C14*50.93	=D14*63.66	=E14*50.93	=B33+C33-E33	=D33-F33	=$H$32*1.05	=G33-H33	=G33/D33	=I33/D33
November	=E33	=C15*50.93	=D15*63.66	=E15*50.93	=B34+C34-E34	=D34-F34	=$H$32*1.05	=G34-H34	=G34/D34	=I34/D34
December	=E34	=C16*50.93	=D16*63.66	=E16*50.93	=B35+C35-E35	=D35-F35	=$H$32*1.05	=G35-H35	=G35/D35	=I35/D35
	=SUM(B24:B35)	=SUM(C24:C35)	=SUM(D24:D35)	=SUM(E24:E35)	=SUM(F24:F35)	=SUM(G24:G35)	=SUM(H24:H35)	=SUM(I24:I35)	=G36/D36	=I36/D36

Quarter	Production Cost	Sales Price
Qtr 1	48.5	=B39*1.23
Qtr 2	=B39*1.04	=B40*1.23
Qtr 3	=B39*1.06	=B41*1.23
Qtr 4	=B39*1.05	=B42*1.25

This table has been included here to show where the numbers have come from for the calculation of variable costs, sales revenue and closing inventory. You refer to the cells in the formula bu you would need to remember to use 'absolute' referencing where appropriate.

TASK 2.2

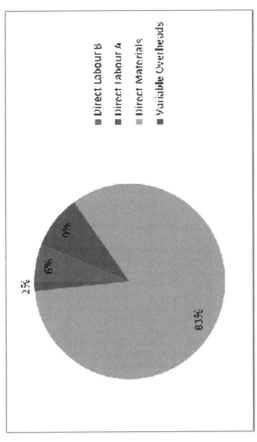

Legend: Direct Labour B · Direct Labour A · Direct Materials · Variable Overheads

Pie chart: 83%, 6%, 9%, 2%

Variable Costs Quarter 1 20X4

Date	Direct Labour B	Direct Labour A	Direct Materials	Variable Overheads	Total
02/01/2014			£172,538.60		£172,538.60
05/01/2014			£95,804.56	£14,800.00	£110,604.56
09/01/2014			£92,119.77		£92,119.77
12/01/2014			£147,486.72		£147,486.72
16/01/2014			£99,636.74		£99,636.74
16/01/2014			£121,223.33		£121,223.33
16/01/2014			£179,440.10		£179,440.10
30/01/2014	£39,822.92	£56,548.54			£96,371.45
05/02/2014			£126,072.27	£12,300.00	£138,372.27
06/02/2014			£78,036.98		£78,036.98
07/02/2014			£112,077.80		£112,077.80
11/02/2014			£103,622.21		£103,622.21
27/02/2014	£45,201.42	£64,186.02			£109,387.44
27/02/2014			£81,189.68		£81,189.68
05/03/2014				£11,100.00	£11,100.00
06/03/2014			£131,115.16		£131,115.16
08/03/2014			£107,767.10		£107,767.10
12/03/2014			£88,576.70		£88,576.70
14/03/2014			£159,521.64		£159,521.64
14/03/2014			£79,597.72		£79,597.72
15/03/2014			£136,359.76		£136,359.76
30/03/2014	£73,736.19	£104,705.39			£178,441.58
	£158,760.53	£225,439.95	£2,112,186.87	£38,200.00	£2,534,587.34
Average			£117,343.71		
Median			£109,922.45		

If your costs don't match make sure you have only included Jan to Mar in the table as we only want the details for the first quarter.

TASK 2.2 CONTINUED

	A	B	C	D	E
1	Sales Outlet	Handbags	Clutch Bags	Shoulder Bags	Total
2	Internet	330	268	948	1546
3	Factory Shop	258	785	630	1673
4	Factory Shop	258	268	967	1493
5	Internet	316	780	967	2063
6	Internet	794	1019	989	2802
7	Retail	258	740	954	1952
8	Factory Shop	938	458	514	1910
9	Internet	698	601	357	1656
10	Factory Shop	842	601	620	2063
11	Retail	623	867	514	2004
12	Factory Shop	867	536	832	2235
13	Internet	757	979	258	1994
14	Factory Shop	393	600	635	1628
15	Retail	391	432	868	1691
16	Factory Shop	758	961	879	2598
17	Internet	879	797	512	2188
18	Retail	698	960	381	2039
19	Internet	498	1036	280	1814
20	Factory Shop	380	380	745	1505
21	Internet	979	1092	740	2811
22	Factory Shop	258	82	502	842
23	Retail	380	258	907	1545
24	Internet	380	960	270	1610
25	Factory Shop	366	499	380	1245
26	Internet	598	1380	895	2873
27	Factory Shop	313	108	501	922

Income by bag type

	Values		
Sales Outlet ▾	Sum o	Sum of Clutch Bags	Sum of Shoulder Bags
Factory Shop	5631	5278	7205
Internet	6229	8912	6216
Retail	2350	3257	3624
Grand Total	14210	17447	17045

Income by outlet

Sum of Total

Sales Outlet ↓	Total
Internet	21357
Factory Shop	18114
Retail	9231
Grand Total	48702

Section 7

SAMPLE ASSESSMENT 2 – QUESTIONS

PART 1

TASK 1.1   (15 marks)

This task is based on a workplace scenario separate to the rest of the assessment.

An accountant, Wajid, has recently started work at Hook Ltd, a large organisation with many employees. He is trying to apply the ethical code's conceptual framework to an ethical problem he is facing at work. He is currently evaluating threats to his fundamental principles.

(a)   **Complete the following statement.**   (2 marks)

To resolve the matter the conceptual framework states that Wajid must use…

▽

▽ Drop down list for task 1.1 (a)

the advice of a lawyer.
his professional judgement.
his common sense.

Sherie is an accountant who works for Hook Ltd. Jorge is a new trainee accountant with Hook Ltd. Sherie tells Jorge that sometimes there is a conflict to be resolved between an individual's personal values and the behaviour of their employer. Sherie personally values loyalty and fairness highly.

(b)   **For each of the following examples identify whether there is a conflict to be resolved between the behaviour of Hook Ltd's management and Sherie's personal values.**
                                                                    (2 marks)

Example of behaviour of Hook Ltd's management	Sherie's personal value	Is there a conflict to resolve?
Long-standing employees are allowed an extra half day's holiday for every two years to permanent employment with Hook Ltd	Loyalty	**Yes/No**
Employees are promoted on the basis of family or other close relationships	Fairness	**Yes/No**

A potential customer of Hook Ltd has asked Sherie to reveal confidential information about Hook Ltd's cost structure and pricing strategy. The potential customer has offered to pay Sherie for this information.

(c) **Identify whether the following statements are true or false.** **(3 marks)**

Statement	True	False
Sherie may never disclose confidential information to any third party.		
The threat that Sherie is facing to her compliance with the fundamental principles is a self-interest threat.		
Sherie must resign immediately from Hook Ltd as her integrity has been compromised by the offer from the potential customer.		

Ian is also an accountant with Hook Ltd. The manager of one of Hook Ltd's main suppliers has offered Ian gifts. Ian has known the manager for several years.

(d) **Complete the following statement** **(2 marks)**

Being offered gifts by the manager is [∇] to Ian's fundamental

principle of [∇]

∇ Drop down lists for task 1.1 (d)

an intimidation threat	objectivity.
a familiarity threat	professional competence and due care.

Ian is following the conflict resolution process in the ethical code in respect of an ethical dilemma at work. Ian has collected evidence and documented the process carefully so he can seek guidance on the dilemma from his friend Antoine, an accountant who works for another organisation.

(e) **Complete the following statement** **(2 marks)**

In relation to the evidence and documentation, Ian must be particularly careful to

ensure the fundamental principle of [∇] Is not

breached when seeking guidance from Antoine.

∇ Drop down list for task 1.1 (e)

confidentiality
professional competence and due care
professional behaviour

Ellie is an accountant who works for a professional accountancy firm. She has a client who has been involved in concealing criminal property. Ellie has reported the client to the relevant authority, and has told the client about this.

(f)   Complete the following statement   **(2 marks)**

Ellie has committed the criminal offence of

∇ Drop down list for task 1.1 (f)

money laundering
failure to disclose
tipping off

Luke is an accountant in practice, working as a sole practitioner. He has discovered that a client has been money laundering.

(g)   Complete the following statement   **(2 marks)**

Luke should disclose confidential information on this matter directly to

∇ Drop down list for task 1.1 (g)

The Money Laundering Reporting Officer.
The National Crime Agency.
HMRC.

END OF TASK

TASK 1.2 (15 marks)

This task is based on the workplace scenario of NewPlace.

Today's date is 15 April 20X7.

You are checking the non-current assets register. A vehicle acquired on 1 January was recorded as a van at £10,000 cost. You find the related purchased invoice.

To: NewPlace 200-210 Farm Road Endsleigh EN1 7DS	From: Car Sales Ltd 178 Judd Road Endsleigh EN62 8SP	Date and tax point: 01 January 20X7 Invoice CJL 69840 VAT 132 5895 01 GB
		£
1.6 litre car VY12 ALK	Purchase Order 584	10,000.00
	VAT at 20%	2,000.00
	Total	12,000.00
Delivery date: 01/01/X7		

You establish that

- the vehicle is a company car for the sales manager's private and business use

- in the ledger accounts the purchase was entered as:

Account	Debit £	Credit £
Vehicles at cost	10,000.00	
VAT	2,000.00	
Bank		12,000.00

- The £2,000 VAT on the purchase of the car should have been recorded as part of the vehicle's cost, not as VAT.

(a) **Show the entries that need to be made in the general ledger to correct the £2,000 VAT that was reclaimed.**

Make each selection by clicking on a box in the left column and then on one in the right column. You can remove a line by clicking on it. (2 marks)

Account
Bank
Depreciation charges
Disposals of non-current assets
Suspense
VAT
Vehicles accumulated depreciation
Vehicles at cost
Vehicles running expenses

Debit £2,000.00
Credit £2,000.00

The entries that you prepared in (a) have not yet been made in the general ledger. You tell Mo that they must be made because recording the £2,000 on the car in the VAT account is not allowed under regulations relating to VAT. However, Mo does not want to make the entries you have prepared. You are aware that this is a serious breach of VAT regulations.

You consider consulting a technical helpline set up by your local college to determine what you should do next.

(b) **According to the ethical code, which of your fundamental principles would be under threat if you called the helpline?** **(1 mark)**

Objectivity	
Confidentiality	

You decide not to consult the technical helpline so you must now consider your position with regards to the ethical code.

(c) **Do you need to take further action to ensure your compliance with the ethical code in this case?** **(2 marks)**

No, no further action by me is necessary because it is Mo's responsibility to decide how to proceed.	
Yes, I should inform Mo in writing that my professional principles prevent me from being connected with a breach of VAT regulations.	
Yes, I am obliged to inform tax authorities about the error myself.	

Mo has now agreed to include the £2,000 as part of the cost of the car in the ledger accounts.

You are recording the annual depreciation charge for the new car. Vehicles are depreciated at 25% per year on a diminishing balance basis.

(d) **Answer to following:**

(i) **Prepare the journal for the first full year's depreciation on the car based on its corrected cost in the general ledger.** **(4 marks)**

Journal

		Dr £	Cr £
	▽		
	▽		

∇ Drop down list for task 1.2 (d) (i)

Administration expenses
Bank
Depreciation charges
Disposals of non-current assets
Purchases
Purchases ledger control account
Sales
Sales ledger control account
Suspense
VAT
Vehicle running expenses
Vehicles accumulated depreciation
Vehicles at costs
<empty>

(ii) **Complete the table to show the effect of adjusting the VAT and depreciation on each of the following.** **(2 marks)**

	Decreased	Increased
Profit for the year		
Carrying amount of non-current assets as at the year end		

(e) **Why might NewPlace choose the diminishing balance method of depreciation for vehicles?** **(2 marks)**

So that the carrying value is always equal to their market value	
To ensure that a profit will be achieved when each vehicle is sold	
To follow the accruals basis of accounting	

Kiera Jackson at Addo & Co believes she has reason to suspect that money laundering has occurred at NewPlace.

(f) **What should Kiera do next?** **(2 marks)**

Discuss the matter in full with Mo	
Make a Suspicious Activity Report to the relevant external authority, detailing her suspicions	
Make an internal report with Addo & Co detailing her suspicions	

TASK 1.3   **(15 marks)**

This task is based on the workplace scenario of NewPlace.

Today's date is 28 February 20X8.

You help to record invoices from NewPlace's suppliers and also to make payments to them. You are aware that all phone calls on the NewPlace office phone are recorded.

DJ Furniture (DJ) is a supplier for NewPlace. Janey Greene is the financial director at DJ. She has telephoned your office several times during February. Each time she has said that DJ has cash flow difficulties and asked you when certain large invoices will be paid. Each time you have replied that all invoices will be paid when they become due, in line with NewPlace procedures.

On 21 February you received a call on your private mobile phone from Janey. She offered you tickets for an expensive event. You said you weren't sure if you could attend, and ended the call.

On 27 February you received another private call from Janey, demanding that you immediately pay an invoice that was not yet due. She said that if you refused she would tell Mo that you demanded expensive tickets from her for making early payments.

(a)   (i)   Describe TWO threats to your ethical principles from Janey's actions.   (2 marks)

(ii)   Describe TWO actions you could take in order to work within the ethical code.

(2 marks)

Threat 1

```
```

Threat 2

```
```

Action 1

```
```

Action 2

Your role at New Place includes:

- supporting sustainability throughout the business

- measuring sustainability in the business.

(b)   Give ONE reason why sustainability is important.

You receive the following email from Mo Hussain:

To: Chris Makepeace Chris.Makepeace@NewPlace.co.uk

From: Mo Hussain Mo.Hussaine@NewPlace.co.uk

Date: 28/2/X8

Hello Chris

I know you are finalising the statement of profit or loss and the statement of financial position for NewPlace for the year ended 31 December 20X7. I would like to know more about the accounting principles they are based on, and how the two statements link together. Also, an accountant friend of mine was telling me about the fundamental qualitative characteristics of useful financial information the other day, but I didn't understand.

I would like you to do the following:

(1)   Describe the TWO key assumptions that underlie the preparation of financial statements, using a relevant example in each case.

(2)   Describe ONE of the two fundamental qualitative characteristics of useful financial information.

(3)   Explain what the statement of financial position tells me.

(4)   Explain ONE way in which the statement of financial position links with the statement of profit or loss.

As I am not an accountant, I would be grateful if you could communicate your responses in a clear manner.

Regards,
Mo

(c) **Reply to Mo, addressing all four points that he has raised.** **(10 marks)**

To:	Mo Hussain Mo.Hussaine@NewPlace.co.uk
From:	Chris Makepeace Chris.Makepeace@NewPlace.co.uk
Date:	28/2/X8

Subject:

PART 2

TASK 2.1 (25 marks)

Download the assessment file

The spreadsheet file includes all questions and data required for this task.

Download the spreadsheet file **"AAT Sample assessment 2 – Assessment book and data – Task 2.1"** from the assessment environment.

1   Save the spreadsheet file in the appropriate location and rename it in the following format: 'your initial-surname-AAT no-dd.mm.yy-Task2.1'.

   For example: J-Donnovan-123456-12.03.xx-Task2.1

2   Follow the instructions within, which provide the full details for each task.

3   Before you proceed to the next task, **save close and upload your completed spreadsheet** using the upload files button.

Complete the tasks in the assessment

Below is a checklist for each task in this assessment.

As you complete each task, tick it off the list to show your progress.

Check boxes are provided for your assistance, using them does not constitute formal evidence that a task has been completed.

		Completed
Part (a)		
Current budget: 'Dec 20X8' worksheet	(7 marks)	
Part (b)		
Revised budget and freezing: 'Revised' worksheet	(5 marks)	
Part (c)		
Profit/loss pro-forma in 'Revised' worksheet	(6 marks)	
Part (d)		
Units to sell in 'Revised' worksheet	(2 marks)	
Part (e)		
Percentage and IF calculations in 'Revised' worksheet	(5 marks)	

SUBMIT THE EVIDENCE REQUIRED

TASK 2.2 **(30 marks)**

Download the assessment file

The spreadsheet file includes all questions and data required for this task.

Download the spreadsheet file **"AAT Sample assessment 2 – Assessment book and data – Task 2.2"** from the assessment environment.

1   Save the spreadsheet file in the appropriate location and rename it in the following format: 'your initial-surname-AAT no-dd.mm.yy-Task2.2'.

For example: J-Donnovan-123456-12.03.xx-Task2.1

2   When the task requires you to import a .txt file, download the file **"AAT Sample assessment 2 – Assessment data (.txt) – Task 2.2"**

3   Follow the instructions within, which provide the full details for each task.

4   Before you proceed to the next task, **save close and upload your completed spreadsheet** using the upload files button.

Complete the tasks in the assessment

Below is a checklist for each task in this assessment.

As you complete each task, tick it off the list to show your progress.

Check boxes are provided for your assistance, using them does not constitute formal evidence that a task has been completed.

		Completed
Part (a) Inventory quantity and value in 'Summary' worksheet	(4 marks)	
Part (b) Pivot chart and table in 'NFS Inventory' worksheet	(5 marks)	
Part (c) Data validation in 'Summary' worksheet	(6 marks)	
Part (d) Import and subtotal – complete ETB	(11 marks)	
Part (e) Locate errors	(4 marks)	

SUBMIT THE EVIDENCE REQUIRED.

Section 8

SAMPLE ASSESSMENT 2 – ANSWERS

PART 1

TASK 1.1 (15 marks)

(a) **Complete the following statement** (2 marks)

To resolve the matter the conceptual framework states that Wajid must use…

his professional judgement. ∇

(b) **Identify whether there is a conflict to be resolved** (2 marks)

Example of behaviour of Hook Ltd's management	Sherie's personal value	Is there a conflict to resolve?
Long-standing employees are allowed an extra half day's holiday for every two years to permanent employment with Hook Ltd	Loyalty	No ∇
Employees are promoted on the basis of family or other close relationships	Fairness	Yes ∇

(c) **Identify whether the following statements are true or false** (3 marks)

Statement	True	False
Sherie may never disclose confidential information to any third party.		✓
The threat that Sherie is facing to her compliance with the fundamental principles is a self-interest threat.	✓	
Sherie must resign immediately from Hook Ltd as her integrity has been compromised by the offer from the potential customer.		✓

(d) **Complete the following statement** (2 marks)

Being offered gifts by the manager is | a familiarity threat ∇ | to Ian's fundamental

principle of | objectivity ∇ |

(e)   **Complete the following statement**   **(2 marks)**

In relation to the evidence and documentation, Ian must be particularly careful to

ensure the fundamental principle of | confidentiality   ▽ | Is not breached

when seeking guidance from Antoine.

(f)   **Complete the following statement**   **(2 marks)**

Ellie has committed the criminal offence of | tipping off.   ▽ |

(g)   **Complete the following statement**   **(2 marks)**

Luke should disclose confidential information on this matter directly to

| the National Crime Agency.   ▽ |

TASK 1.2   (16 marks)

(a)   **Show the entries that need to be made in the general ledger to correct the £2,000 VAT that was reclaimed.**   **(2 marks)**

	Account
	Bank
Debit £2,000.00	Depreciation charges
	Disposals of non-current assets
	Suspense
Credit £2,000.00	VAT
	Vehicles accumulated depreciation
	Vehicles at cost
	Vehicles running expenses

(b)   **According to the ethical code, which of your fundamental principles would be under threat if you called the helpline?**   **(1 mark)**

Objectivity	
Confidentiality	✓

(c)   **Do you need to take further action to ensure your compliance with the ethical code in this case?**   **(2 marks)**

No, no further action by me is necessary because it is Mo's responsibility to decide how to proceed.	
Yes, I should inform Mo in writing that my professional principles prevent me from being connected with a breach of VAT regulations.	✓
Yes, I am obliged to inform tax authorities about the error myself.	

(d) **Answer to following:**

(i) Prepare the journal for the first full year's depreciation on the car based on its corrected cost in the general ledger. **(4 marks)**

Journal

		Dr £	Cr £
Depreciation charges	▽	3,000	
Vehicles accumulated depreciation	▽		3,000

(ii) Complete the table to show the effect of adjusting the VAT and depreciation on each of the following. **(2 marks)**

	Decreased	Increased
Profit for the year	✓	
Carrying amount of non-current assets as at the year end		✓

(e) Why might NewPlace choose the diminishing balance method of depreciation for vehicles? **(2 marks)**

So that the carrying value is always equal to their market value	
To ensure that a profit will be achieved when each vehicle is sold	
To follow the accruals basis of accounting	✓

(f) **What should Kiera do next?** **(2 marks)**

Discuss the matter in full with Mo	
Make a Suspicious Activity Report to the relevant external authority, detailing her suspicions	
Make an internal report with Addo & Co detailing her suspicions	✓

TASK 1.3 (15 marks)

(a) **Threat 1**

> Janey's offer of expensive hospitality is a self-interest threat to my ethical principle of objectivity/integrity/professional behaviour. (1)
>
> A self-interest threat occurs when a financial or other interest will inappropriately influence an accountant's judgement or behaviour.

Threat 2

> Janey's last call is an intimidation threat to objectivity. (1)
>
> An intimidation threat occurs when an accountant may be deterred from acting objectively by threats, whether actual or perceived. The original offer from her was not recorded so she could conceivably claim that I demanded the tickets.

Actions I should take

> Reference can be made to any one of the following (maximum two marks)
>
> - Use Conceptual Framework OR conflict resolution process from Code (1)
>
> - Follow any relevant internal procedure (1)
>
> - Disclose/seek advice internally or from AAT (1)
>
> - Reject offer of tickets (1)
>
> - Continue to follow normal procedure (1)

(b) It is important to take a long term view and allow the needs of present generations to be met without compromising the ability of future generations to meet their needs (1).

(c) *An example of 10 mark submission. Students are not expected to raise all the points below for the full 10 marks, but their inclusion here serves to indicate the depth of knowledge required for each item.*

To:	Mo Hussain Mo.Hussaine@NewPlace.co.uk
From:	Chris Makepeace Chris.Makepeace@NewPlace.co.uk
Date:	28/2/X8

Subject: | Accounting principles and financial information

Thank you for your email of 28/2/X8

(1)
> Two key assumptions:
>
> Accrual/matching basis of accounting: we include transactions in the accounting period when they arise, not when they are paid in the form of cash.
>
> For instance the 20X7 financial statements will include some items of inventory even though we have not yet paid the invoices from their suppliers.
>
> Going concern assumption: we assume that the business will continue in operation for the foreseeable future, without the need to sell assets and pay liabilities at short notice.
>
> If we did not assume this, the amounts we show for non-current assets, for example, would be different (market or 'fire sale' value rather than how much they cost when they were bought less depreciation).

(2)

EITHER

Relevance: financial information is relevant to the user if it is can make a difference to decisions made by the user. The information might be able to help them make decisions by predicting future outcomes (it has predictive value) or by confirming or changing their previous evaluations (it has confirmatory value).

OR

Faithful (re)presentation: the financial information is complete (it includes all necessary descriptions and explanations), neutral (without bias in how it is selected or presented) and free from error (no errors or omissions).

(3)

The statement of financial position (SFP) lists out your business's assets less its liabilities (including loans), so you can see how much the business is worth (its net asset value). It then shows how the net assets are funded – which is by your capital: the amounts you have introduced into the business plus the profits you have made and kept in the business.

(4)

The SFP links with the statement of profit or loss (SOPOL) via the profit figure. In the SOPOL the business's costs are deducted from its revenue to arrive at the profit for the period. In the SFP this figure is added to the capital you had in the business at the start of the period. Any amounts you have withdrawn in the period for your own use are deducted from this figure to arrive at your total capital.

OR

The SFP links with the statement of profit or loss (SOPOL) via the closing inventory figure. In the SOPOL the cost of closing inventory is deducted from the business's costs for 20X7. This is because its cost needs to be deducted from the revenue 20X8, when the inventory is actually sold. Instead the inventory is shown as an asset in the SFP for 20X7 to be carried forward and matched with revenue in 20X8.

Kind regards

Chris

PART 2

TASK 2.1 (25 marks)

Note to candidate:
Please ensure you upload this spreadsheet before the end of the assessment. If you do not upload your work, it will not be marked.

(a)

NewPlace: Current budgeted performance data for six months to 31 December 20X8

	A	B	C
4	Sales volume (units)	10000	
5	Average selling price per unit	£165	
6	Average cost per unit	£125	
7	Wages of shop staff	£102,500	
8	Rent and rates	£85,000	
9	Administration overheads	£62,500	
10	Depreciation	£75,000	

Assessor - formulas used in all column C e.g. to calculate Sales =B4*B5

NewPlace: Current budgeted net profit/loss for six months ended 31 December 20X8

	A	B	C
12		£	£
13	Sales		£1,650,000
14	Cost of sales:		
15	Cost of goods for resale	£1,250,000	£1,250,000
16			£400,000
17	Gross profit		
18	Wages of shop staff	£102,500	
19	Rent and rates	£85,000	
20	Administration overheads	£62,500	
21	Depreciation	£75,000	£325,000
22			
23	Net profit/loss for the six months		£75,000

Assessor this cell should show £1,650,000 using a formula

Assessor - this cell should show a profit of £75,000 using a formula

Revised worksheet

	A	B	C	D	...
1	(b)				
2	NewPlace: Budgeted performance data for six months to 31				
3	December 20X8	Original	Revised		
4	Sales volume (units)	10000	11000	*Assessor - this cell should have a formula in it showing 11,000*	
5	Average selling price per unit	£165.00	£174.00	*Assessor this cell should show £174.00 and have the formula =ROUNDUP(B5*1.05,0)*	
6	Average cost per unit	£125.00	£125.00		
7	Wages of shop staff	£102,500.00	£122,500.00	*Assessor - this cell should show £122,500.00 with a formula =B7+40000/2*	
8	Rent and rates	£85,000.00	£85,000.00		
9	Administration overheads	£62,500.00	£65,000.00	*Assessor this cell should show £65,000.00 with a formula =B9+2500*	
10	Depreciation	£75,000.00	£75,000.00		
11					
12					
13	(c)				
14	NewPlace: Revised budgeted net profit/loss for six months ended 31 December 20X8	£	£		
15	Sales		£1,914,000	*Assessor this cell should show £1,914,000*	
16	Cost of sales:				
17	Cost of goods for resale	£1,375,000			
18			£1,375,000		
19	Gross profit		£539,000		
20	Wages of shop staff	£122,500		*Assessor - make sure this figure only includes 6 months of extra staff costs*	
21	Rent and rates	£85,000			
22	Administration overheads	£65,000			
23	Depreciation	£75,000			
24			£347,500		
25	Net profit/loss for the six months		£191,500	*Assessor - this cell should be a formula and show a profit of £191,500*	
26					
27	(d)				
28	Revised contribution per unit		£49.00		
29	Units required to achieve target net profit		12,500	*Assessor - this cell should show a formula =(265000+C24)/C28*	
30					
31	(e)				
32	Percentage change in revised budgeted sales	16.00%	Bonus to be paid	*Assessor this cell should show "Bonus to be paid" and have the formula =IF(B29>=15%,"Bonus to be paid","No bonus")*	
33	Percentage change in revised budgeted net profit/loss	155.33%		*Assessor the contents of B32 and B33 should be formulas and formatted to percentage to 2 decimal places*	
34					
35					
36					
37					

Bonus

Note to candidate: Please ensure you upload this spreadsheet before the end of the assessment. If you do not upload your work, it will not be marked.

Assessor - ensure that you cannot scroll above row 11 or into columns A,B or C

TASK 2.2 (30 marks)

NFS Inventory worksheet

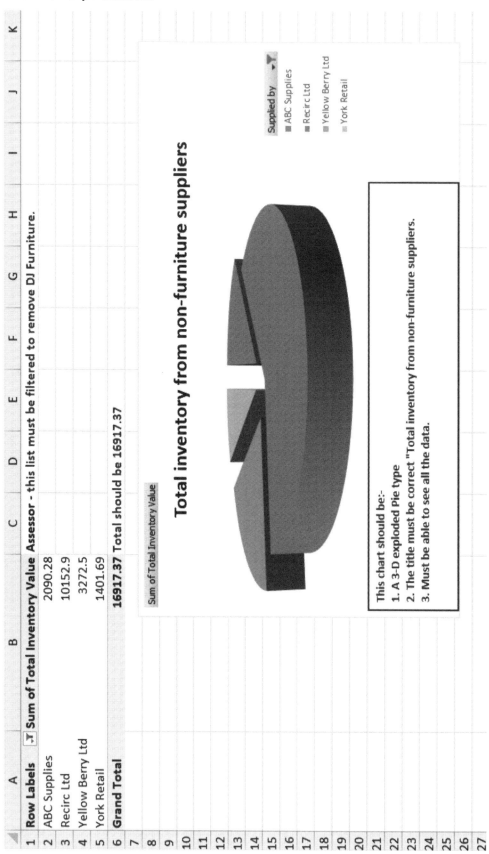

	A	B
1	**Row Labels**	**Sum of Total Inventory Value**
2	ABC Supplies	2090.28
3	Recirc Ltd	10152.9
4	Yellow Berry Ltd	3272.5
5	York Retail	1401.69
6	**Grand Total**	**16917.37**

Assessor – this list must be filtered to remove DJ Furniture.

Total should be 16917.37

Sum of Total Inventory Value

Total inventory from non-furniture suppliers

Supplied by

■ ABC Supplies
■ Recirc Ltd
■ Yellow Berry Ltd
■ York Retail

This chart should be:-
1. A 3-D exploded Pie type
2. The title must be correct "Total inventory from non-furniture suppliers.
3. Must be able to see all the data.

Summary worksheet

	A	B	C	D	E	F	G	H	I	J	K	L	M	N
1														
2	Summary of Inventory						Approved Suppliers list							
	Item description	Total Quantity	Cost per item	Total Value	Supplied by									
3	10 draw filing cab grey	52	£899.00	£46,748.00	DJ Furniture		Yellow Berry Ltd				**Assessor** - Rows 1 and 2 should be			
4	15 draw fining cab grey	36	£1,118.00	£40,248.00	DJ Furniture		ABC Supplies				frozen - you should not be able to scroll			
5	2 drawer filing cab grey	60	£276.00	£16,560.00	DJ Furniture		York Retail				above here.			
6	3 drawer desk Glass top	32	£572.00	£18,304.00	DJ Furniture		Recirc Ltd							
7	4 drawer desk glass top	12	£350.00	£4,200.00	DJ Furniture		DJ Furniture							
8	4 drawer filing cab lock black	21	£268.00	£5,628.00	DJ Furniture									
9	6 door storage locker	9	£230.00	£2,070.00	DJ Furniture						**Assessor:** cells G3: G7 should be protected			
10	6 door storage locker w/locks	14	£258.00	£3,612.00	DJ Furniture									
11	A3 ream blue 100g	80	£2.60	£208.00	Yellow Berry Ltd									
12	A3 ream blue 80g	66	£2.50	£165.00	Yellow Berry Ltd						**Assessor** - Cells in the range E3:E75 must be data validated.			
13	A3 ream bright white 80g	121	£2.20	£266.20	Yellow Berry Ltd						They must show a drop down box if any cell in that range is selected.			
14	A3 ream bright white100g	78	£2.60	£202.80	Yellow Berry Ltd						The drop down box must say "Please choose from the drop down list"			
15	A3 ream white 100g	85	£2.20	£187.00	Yellow Berry Ltd						When you select any cell drop down box you should only see the supplier list shown in G3:G7			
16	A3 ream white 80g	57	£2.10	£119.70	Yellow Berry Ltd									
17	A3 ream yellow 100g	119	£2.60	£309.40	Yellow Berry Ltd									
18	A3 ream yellow 80g	94	£2.50	£235.00	Yellow Berry Ltd									
19	A4 ream blue 100g	88	£2.40	£211.20	Yellow Berry Ltd									
20	A4 ream blue 80g	97	£2.20	£213.40	Yellow Berry Ltd									
21	A4 ream blue card 250g	32	£2.90	£92.80	York Retail									
22	A4 ream bright white 100g	109	£1.90	£207.10	Yellow Berry Ltd									
23	A4 ream bright white 80g	132	£1.80	£237.60	Yellow Berry Ltd									

57	Paper clips 40mm (100)	38	£0.59	£22.42	ABC Supplies
58	Paper clips extra large (100)	31	£2.40	£74.40	ABC Supplies
59	Pedestal 2 draw black	24	£195.00	£4,680.00	DJ Furniture
60	Pedestal 3 draw black	32	£280.00	£8,960.00	DJ Furniture
61	Pedestal 3 draw oak effect	35	£350.00	£12,250.00	DJ Furniture
62	Pen Black pack of 5	82	£1.51	£123.82	York Retail
63	Pen Red pack of 5	105	£1.51	£158.55	York Retail
64	Pencil 2B pack of 10	101	£1.98	£199.98	York Retail
65	Pencil H pack of 10	107	£1.98	£211.86	York Retail
66	Pencil sharpener Black	41	£0.59	£24.19	ABC Supplies
67	Pencil sharpener Red	61	£0.59	£35.99	ABC Supplies
68	Ruler non splinter 30cm	27	£0.59	£15.93	York Retail
69	Ruler steel 30cm	33	£1.89	£62.37	York Retail
70	Scissors 15cm black	27	£5.65	£152.55	York Retail
71	Scissors 15cm black left hand	25	£6.85	£171.25	York Retail
72	Stapler size 41 Blue	81	£6.21	£503.01	ABC Supplies
73	Stapler size 41 Red	31	£6.21	£192.51	ABC Supplies
74	Storage box 20x35x12 Black	35	£3.48	£121.80	ABC Supplies
75	Storage box 20x35x12 Red	21	£2.56	£53.76	ABC Supplies
76	**Total value in inventory**			£200,132.72	
77					
78					
79					
80					
81					
82					
83					

Assessor: cells in column D should show formula e.g. =B64*C64

Assessor - this cell should contain a formula =SUM(D3:D75) and a value of £200,132.72

Assessor - cells in this column must have a linked formula = 'Store 1'!B75+'Store 2'!B75+'Store 3'!B75

ETB Worksheet

NewPlace: Extended trial balance for the year 20X8

Account name	Ledger balances Dr	Ledger balances Cr	Adjustments Dr	Adjustments Cr	Statement of profit or loss Dr	Statement of profit or loss Cr	Statement of Financial position Dr	Statement of Financial position Cr
Cash at bank	£ 12,780						£ 12,780	
Cash in hand	£ 3,450						£ 3,450	
Sales		£ 3,850,400				£ 3,850,400		
Capital		£ 364,810						£ 364,810
Purchases – goods for resale 1	£ 905,840				£ 905,840			
Purchases – goods for resale 2	£ 529,700				£ 529,700			
Purchases – goods for resale 3	£ 1,342,460		2,780		£ 1,345,240			
Shop wages grade 1	£ 98,740				£ 98,740			
Shop wages grade 2	£ 137,760				£ 137,760			
Rent total	£ 140,000				£ 140,000			
Rates total	£ 32,000			1,450	£ 32,000			
Administration costs	£ 84,670				£ 83,220			
Administration salaries	£ 45,210				£ 45,210			
Non-current assets	£ 920,000						£ 920,000	
Depreciation expense			£ 150,000	£ 150,000	£ 150,000			
Accumulated depreciation		£ 450,000						£ 600,000
Purchase ledger control		£ 231,500						£ 231,500
Other payables – accruals				£ 2,780				£ 2,780
Sales ledger control	£ 415,600						£ 415,600	
Allowance for doubtful debts				£ 2,000				£ 2,000
Irrecoverable debts expense			£ 2,000		£ 2,000			
Other receivables – prepaid			£ 1,450				£ 1,450	
Inventory	£ 178,500		£ 182,700	£ 182,700	£ 178,500		£ 182,700	
Drawings	£ 50,000						£ 50,000	
Profit					£ 384,890			£ 384,890
	£ 4,896,710	£ 4,896,710	£ 338,930	£ 338,930	£ 4,033,100	£ 4,033,100	£ 1,585,980	£ 1,585,980

Assessor: Check that cells B11:B15 and cells B18:B19 are linked to Subtotal worksheet - e.g. =Subtotal!E4

Assessor: Check that cells B16 and B17 are linked to Subtotal worksheet - e.g. =Subtotal!F18 and =Subtotal!F23

Assessor: changes to be made to cells F18 and I23/24

Assessor to check format of currency with zero decimals, and all contents seen (a)

Assessor to check that F31 and I31 have the correct amount entered (b)

Subtotal worksheet

	A	B	C	D	E	F
4				Purchases - goods for resale 1	905840	
5				Purchases - goods for resale 2	529700	
6				Purchases - goods for resale 3	1342460	
7				Shop wages grade 1	98740	
8				Shop wages grade 2	137760	
9				Administration costs	84670	
10				Administration salaries	45210	
13				Item	Shop	Cost
14				Rent	Shop 1	21000
15				Rent	Shop 2	25600
16				Rent	Shop 3	35200
17				Rent	Shop 4	58200
18				**Rent Total**		140000
19				Rates	Shop 1	4800
20				Rates	Shop 2	5850
21				Rates	Shop 3	8050
22				Rates	Shop 4	13300
23				**Rates Total**		32000
24				**Grand Total**		172000

Assessor - check that this cell contains the formula =SUBTOTAL(9,F14:F17)